Working Papers

for use with

Managerial Accounting

Tenth Edition

Ray H. Garrison, D.B.A., CPA
Professor Emeritus
Brigham Young University

Eric W. Noreen, Ph.D., CMA
Professor Emeritus
University of Washington

Prepared by
Jeannie Folk
College of DuPage

Irwin
McGraw-Hill

Boston Burr Ridge, IL Dubuque, IA Madison, WI New York San Francisco St. Louis
Bangkok Bogotá Caracas Lisbon London Madrid
Mexico City Milan New Delhi Seoul Singapore Sydney Taipei Toronto

McGraw-Hill Higher Education

A Division of The ***McGraw-Hill*** *Companies*

Working Papers for use with
MANAGERIAL ACCOUNTING

Printed in the United States of America.

1 2 3 4 5 6 7 8 9 0 QPD/QPD 0 9 8 7 6 5 4 3 2

ISBN 0-07-253176-2

http://www.mhhe.com

Contents

Problem 1-4 Name ______________________

1. Organization chart:

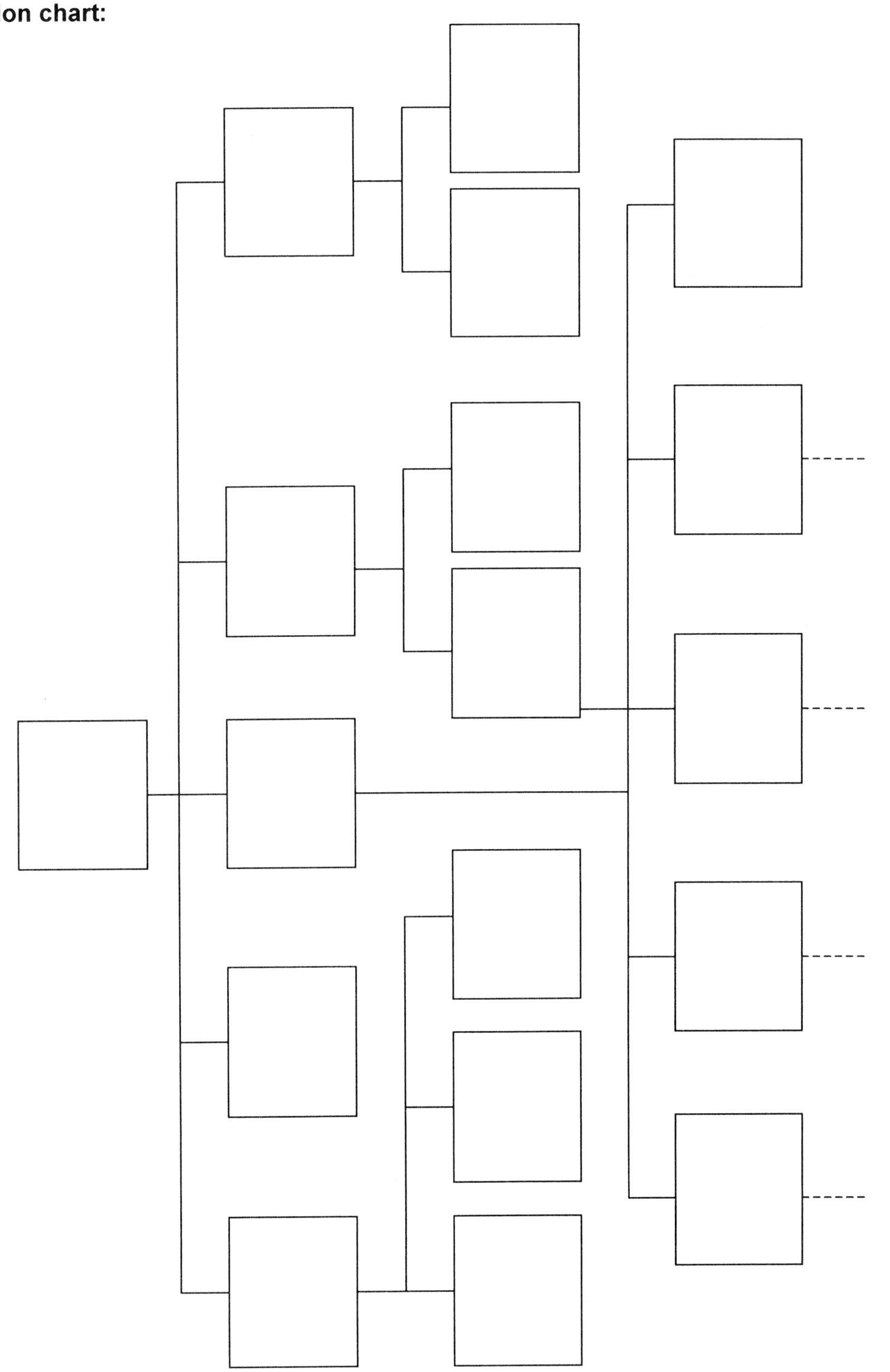

Problem 1-4 (Continued) **Name** ____________________

2. Comments regarding line and staff positions:

3. Positions with a need for accounting information:

Problem 1-5 Name ______________________________

1. Conclusion as to whether Sarver acted ethically:

2. Comments regarding Sarver's justification for his actions:

Problem 1-6 Name Erika Grunwald

1. Definitions of line and staff positions:

Line position - are directly related to achievement of the basic objectives of an organization.

Staff positions are indirectly related to the achievement of the organization's basic objectives. (They support the line positions)

2. Characteristics of line and staff managers that may cause conflicts:

Problem 1-6 (Continued) **Name** ______________________

3. a. and b. Identification, explanation and potential problems for each position:

Problem 1-7 Name Erica Grunwald

1. Relationship between behavior described and customers:

2. Impact of behavior on profits and employment in automotive service industry:

Problem 1-8 Name ______________________

1. Comments supporting ethical responsibility of Williams:

2. Appropriateness of each of the three alternative courses of action:

Problem 1-8 (Continued)   Name ______________________

3. Steps to be taken by Williams:

Group Exercise 1-9 Name

Name ______________________________

Problem 2-11 Name ____________________

Name of the Cost	Variable Cost	Fixed Cost	Product Cost			Period (Selling & Admin.) Cost	Opportunity Cost	Sunk Cost
			Direct Materials	Direct Labor	Mfg. Overhead			

Problem 2-12

Name ______________________________

COST ITEM	COST BEHAVIOR		TO UNITS OF PRODUCT	
	VARIABLE	FIXED	DIRECT	INDIRECT
1. Plastic washers used in auto production				
2. Production superintendent's salary				
3. Laborers assembling a product				
4. Electricity for operation of machines				
5. Janitorial salaries				
6. Clay used in brick production				
7. Rent on a factory building				
8. Wood used in ski production				
9. Screws used in furniture production				
10. A supervisor's salary				
11. Cloth used in suit production				
12. Depreciation of cafeteria equipment				
13. Glue used in textbook production				
14. Lubricants for machines				
15. Paper used in textbook production				

Notes:

Problem 2-13 Name ______________________

1. Total wages and allocation:

2. Total wages and allocation:

3. Total wages and fringe benefits and allocation:

Problem 2-13 (Continued) **Name** ______________________

4. Allocation of wages and fringe benefits:

Problem 2-14 Name ______________________________

1.

YEDDER ENTERPRISES
Quality Cost Report (in thousands of dollars)

	This Year		Last Year	
	Amount	Percent	Amount	Percent

Problem 2-14 (Continued) **Name** ____________________

2. Bar graph of quality costs (in thousands):

Problem 2-14 (Continued) **Name** ______________________

Bar graph of quality costs as a percentage of sales:

Problem 2-14 (Continued) Name ______________________

3. Evaluation of distribution of quality costs:

Problem 2-15 Name ____________________

Cost Item	Variable or Fixed	Selling Cost	Administrative Cost	Manufacturing (Product) Cost	
				Direct	Indirect
1. Depreciation, executive jet					
2. Costs of shipping finished goods to customers					
3. Wood used in furniture manufacturing					
4. Sales manager's salary					
5. Electricity used in furniture manufacturing					
6. Secretary to the company president.					
7. Aerosol attachment placed on a spray can produced by the company					
8. Billing costs					
9. Packing supplies for shipping products overseas					
10. Sand used in concrete manufacturing					
11. Supervisor's salary, factory					
12. Executive life insurance					
13. Sales commissions					
14. Fringe benefits, assembly-line workers					
15. Advertising costs					
16. Property taxes on finished goods warehouses					
17. Lubricants for machines					

Problem 2-16 Name Erika Grunwald

1. Comments regarding viewpoints:

2. Comments regarding president's statement about classification of salary cost:

Problem 2-17 **Name** ____________________

1. Cost classification:

Name of Cost	Variable Cost	Fixed Cost	Product Cost			Period (Selling & Admin.) Cost	Opportunity Cost	Sunk Cost
			Direct Materials	Direct Labor	Mfg. Overhead			

Problem 2-17 (Continued) **Name** ______________________

2. Comments regarding cost that is not a differential cost:

Problem 2-18

Name ______________________

1. Cost classifications:

COST ITEM	COST BEHAVIOR: VARIABLE	COST BEHAVIOR: FIXED	SELLING OR ADM. COST	PRODUCT COST: DIRECT	PRODUCT COST: INDIRECT
Direct materials used (wood And glass)	430000 —			430000 —	
General office salaries		110000 —	110000 —		
Factory supervision					
Sales commissions					
Depreciation, factory building					
Depreciation, office equipment					
Indirect materials, factory					
Factory labor (cutting and assembly)					
Advertising					
Insurance, factory					
General office supplies (billing)					
Property taxes, factory					
Utilities, factory					

2. Average product cost per bookcase:

3. Impact of drop in production on average cost per bookcase:

4.a. Viewpoints regarding the meaning of "cost":

b. Cost term that would justify charging the full, regular price:

Problem 2-19 Name ______________________

1. **MEDCO, INC.**
Schedule of Cost of Goods Manufactured

 Name ______________________

2.

MEDCO, INC.
Income Statement

3. Average cost per unit for direct materials and for factory depreciation:

4. Unit cost and total cost for direct materials and for depreciation:

5. Comments regarding difference in average costs:

Problem 2-20 Name ______________________

1.

SKYLER COMPANY
Schedule of Cost of Goods Manufactured
for the month ended June 30

Problem 2-20 (Continued) Name ______________________

2.

SKYLER COMPANY
Income Statement
for the month ended June 30

3. Recommendation:

Problem 2-21 Name Erika Grunwald

1.

VALENKO COMPANY
Schedule of Cost of Goods Manufactured
for the year ended December 31

 Name ______________________

VALENKO COMPANY
Cost of Goods Section of Income Statement
For the Year Ended December 31

2. Average cost per unit for direct materials and for rent:

3. Unit cost and total cost for direct materials and for rent:

4. Comments regarding difference in average costs:

Problem 2-22 Name Erica Grunwald

1. Conclusion as to whether Richart's actions are ethical:

2. Comments regarding management philosophy and accounting policies:

Problem 2-23 **Name** ____________________

1. Quality cost report:

BERGEN, INC.
Quality Cost Report
(in thousands)

	Year 1		Year 2	
	Amount	Percentage	Amount	Percentage

Problem 2-23 (Continued) **Name** ____________________

Conclusion regarding quality improvement program:

2. Comments regarding Reese's reactions to quality improvement program:

3. Measurement of opportunity cost:

Problem 2-24 Name ____________________

Description	Direct or Indirect Cost of the Immunization Center		Direct or Indirect Cost of Particular Patients		Variable or Fixed with Respect to the Number of Immunizations	
	Direct	Indirect	Direct	Indirect	Variable	Fixed
a. The salary of the head nurse in the Immunization Center						
b. Costs of incidental supplies consumed in the Immunization Center such as paper towels						
c. The cost of lighting and heating the Immunization Center						
d. The cost of disposable syringes used in the Immunization Center						
e. The salary of the Central Area Well-Baby Clinic's Information Systems Manager						
f. The costs of mailing letters soliciting donations to the Central Area Well-Baby Clinic						
g. The wages of nurses who work in the Immunization Center						
h. The cost of medical malpractice insurance for the Central Area Well-Baby Clinic						
i. Depreciation on the fixtures and equipment in the Immunization Center						

Problem 2-25 **Name** ____________________

	Case 1	Case 2	Case 3	Case 4
Direct materials				
Direct labor				
Manufacturing overhead				
Total manufacturing costs				
Beginning work in process inventory				
Ending work in process inventory				
Cost of goods manufactured				
Sales				
Beginning finished goods inventory				
Cost of goods manufactured				
Goods available for sale				
Ending finished goods inventory				
Cost of goods sold				
Gross margin				
Operating expenses				
Net income				

Problem 2-26 Name ____________________

1.

HICKEY COMPANY
Schedule of Cost of Goods Manufactured

2.a. Number of units in ending finished goods inventory:

b. Average production cost per unit:

 Name ______________________

3.

HICKEY COMPANY
Income Statement

Case 2-27 Name ______________________

1. Conceptual errors made in preparation of income statement:

2. MEDICAL TECHNOLOGY, INC.
Schedule of Cost of Goods Manufactured
For the Quarter Ended June 30

Case 2-27 (Continued) Name ______________________

3. Calculation of cost of units in ending finished goods inventory:

MEDICAL TECHNOLOGY, INC.
Corrected Income Statement
For the Quarter Ended June 30

 Name ____________________

4. Comments regarding insurance claim:

Case 2-28 **Name** ______________________

Name ______________________________

Group Exercise 2-29 Name ______________________

1. Explanation of Ford's statements regarding color of Model T:

2. Achievement of further efficiencies:

3. Comments regarding lowering cost of a high-volume, commodity product:

4. Application of concepts described to university education:

Application of concepts described to a stay in a hospital:

Group Exercise 2-30 Name ______________________

1. Definitions of fixed costs and variable costs:

2. Examples of fixed costs and variable costs for a steel company and relevant measures of production activity:

3. Examples of fixed costs and variable costs and relevant measures of production activity for a:

Hospital:

University:

Auto manufacturer:

4. Relationships at a steel company:

Group Exercise 2-30 (Continued) Name ______________________

5. Graph depicting how total costs behave as a function of how many tons of steel are produced:

6. Graph depicting how average costs per unit behave as a function of how many tons of steel are produced:

7. Comments regarding how costs behave with changes in demand once capacity has been set:

Problem 3-13 Name ______________________

1. and 2. Posting of entries to T-accounts:

Cash	

Accounts Receivable	

Raw Materials	

Work in Process	

Finished Goods	

Prepaid Insurance	

Buildings and Equipment	

Accumulated Depreciation	

Manufacturing Overhead	

Accounts Payable	

Retained Earnings	

Capital Stock	

Salaries Expense	

Depreciation Expense	

Insurance Expense	

Shipping Expense	

Cost of Goods Sold	

Sales	

3. Allocation of underapplied or overapplied manufacturing overhead:

Journal entry:

 Name ______________________

4.

FANTASTIC PROPS, INC.
Income Statement
For the Year Ended December 31

Problem 3-14 **Name** ____________________

1. Journal entries:

a.			
b.			
c.			
d.			
e.			
f.			
g.			
h.			
i.			
j.			

Problem 3-14 (Continued) Name ______________________

2. Raw Materials

Manufacturing Overhead

Work in Process

Cost of Goods Sold

Finished Goods

3. Conclusion and journal entry:

4.

RAVSTEN COMPANY
Income Statement
For the Year Ended December 31

Problem 3-15 Name ______________________

1. and 2. Posting of entries to T-accounts:

Cash	

Accounts Receivable	

Raw Materials	

Work in Process	

Finished Goods	

Prepaid Insurance	

Plant and Equipment	

Accumulated Depreciation	

Manufacturing Overhead	

Accounts Payable	

Problem 3-15 (continued) Name ____________________

Salaries & Wages Payable

Retained Earnings

Capital Stock

Sales Commissions Expense

Administrative Salaries Expense

Depreciation Expense

Insurance Expense

Miscellaneous Expense

Cost of Goods Sold

Sales

3. Conclusion and journal entry:

 Name ______________________

4.

DURHAM COMPANY
Income Statement
For the Year Ended December 31

Problem 3-16 Name ______________________________

1. Journal entries:

a.			
b.			
c.			
d.			
e.			
f.			
g.			
h.			
i.			
j.			

 Name ______________

2.

Raw Materials

Work in Process

Finished Goods

Manufacturing Overhead

Cost of Goods Sold

3. Conclusion and journal entry:

4.

SOVEREIGN MILLWORK, INC.
Income Statement
for the Year Ended June 30

Problem 3-17

Name

1.

Raw Materials	

Work in Process	

Finished Goods	

Manufacturing Overhead	

Salaries & Wages Payable	

Accounts Payable	

2. Journal entries:

a.			
b.			
c.			

Problem 3-17 (Continued) **Name** ____________________

3. Predetermined overhead rate:

Journal entry:

4. Total cost of Job 105:

Journal entry:

5. Breakdown of Work in Process account balance:

	Job 106	Job 107	Total

Problem 3-18 **Name** ______________________

1. Predetermined overhead rate:

2. Amount of under- or overapplied overhead for the year:

3. Journal entry:

4. Allocation to Work in Process, Finished Goods, and Cost of Goods Sold:

Journal entry:

5. Difference in cost of goods sold:

Impact on net operating income:

Problem 3-19 **Name** ______________________

1. a. Predetermined overhead rate:

b. Amount of under- or overapplied manufacturing overhead:

Problem 3-19 (Continued) Name ______________________

2.

PACIFIC MANUFACTURING COMPANY
Schedule of Cost of Goods Manufactured

3. Cost of goods sold:

Options available for disposing of under- or overapplied overhead:

 Name ____________________

4. Price charged to customer:

5. Amount of overhead cost in Work in Process:

Amount of direct materials cost in Work in Process:

Completed schedule of costs in Work in Process:

Problem 3-20 Name ______________________

1. Journal entries:

a.			
b.			
c.			
d.			
e.			
f.			
g.			
h.			
i.			
j.			

k.			
l.			
m.			

Problem 3-20 (Continued)

Name ______________________________

2.

Cash	

Accounts Receivable	

Raw Materials	

Work in Process	

Finished Goods	

Prepaid Insurance	

Buildings and Equipment	

Accumulated Depreciation	

Manufacturing Overhead	

Problem 3-20 (Continued) Name ______________________

Salaries & Wages Payable	

Accounts Payable	

Retained Earnings	

Capital Stock	

Marketing Expense	

Depreciation Expense	

Insurance Expense	

Salaries Expense	

Cost of Goods Sold	

Sales	

 Name ______________________

3. Conclusion and journal entry:

4. ALMEDA PRODUCTS, INC.
Income Statement
for the Year Ended December 31

Problem 3-21 Name ______________________

1. Preparation Department predetermined overhead rate:

Fabrication Department predetermined overhead rate:

2. Total overhead cost:

3. Total Cost of Job 127:

	Preparation	Fabrication	Total

4. Under- or overapplied overhead:

	Preparation	Fabrication

Problem 3-22 Name ____________________

1. Research & Documents predetermined overhead rate:

Litigation predetermined overhead rate:

2. Total overhead cost:

3. Total cost of Case 618-3:

	Research & Documents	Litigation	Total

4. Over- or underapplied overhead:

	Research & Documents	Litigation

Problem 3-23 Name ____________________

1. Overhead applied to Slug Fest job:

	2002	2001

Under- or overapplied overhead:

	2002	2001

2. Overhead applied to Slug Fest job:

	2002	2001

Under- or overapplied overhead:

	2002	2001

Problem 3-23 (Continued) Name ______________________

3. Interpretation:

4. Fundamental business problem facing company and recommendation regarding method used to calculate predetermined overhead rate:

Problem 3-24 **Name** ________________

1. Cost of raw materials put into production:

2. Amount of indirect materials put into production:

3. Indirect labor cost:

4. Cost of goods manufactured:

Problem 3-24 (Continued) Name ______________________

5. Cost of goods sold:

6. Predetermined overhead rate:

7. Under- or overapplied manufacturing overhead:

8. Components of ending balance in Work in Process:

Problem 3-25 Name

1. a. Predetermined overhead rate:

b. Amount of manufacturing overhead cost applied to Hastings job:

2. a. Predetermined overhead rates:

	Cutting Department	Machining Department	Assembly Department

b. Total applied overhead:

3. Explanation of difference in amount of overhead applied to Hastings job:

 Name ______________________________

4. Bid price:

Bid price assuming use of departmental overhead rates:

5. a. Under- or overapplied overhead:

Problem 3-25 (Continued) Name ______________________

5b. Under- or overapplied overhead:

	Cutting Dept.	Machining Dept.	Assembly Dept.	Total Plant

Problem 3-26 Name ______________________

1.

Cash	

Accounts Receivable	

Raw Materials	

Work in Process	

Finished Goods	

Prepaid Insurance	

Plant & Equipment	

Accumulated Depreciation	

Manufacturing Overhead	

Accounts Payable	

Problem 3-26 (Continued) Name ______________________

Salaries & Wages Payable	

Retained Earnings	

Capital Stock	

Salaries Expense	

Insurance Expense	

Advertising Expense	

Depreciation Expense	

Miscellaneous Expense	

Cost of Goods Sold	

Sales	

2.

TOP-PRODUCTS, INC.
Schedule of Cost of Goods Manufactured
for the Year Ended December 31

3. Journal entry:

Schedule of cost of goods sold:

 Name ______________________

4. TOP-PRODUCTS, INC.
Income Statement
for the Year Ended December 31

5. Total amount billed and price per unit:

Problem 3-27 Name ______________________

1. Journal entries:

a.			
b.			
c.			
d.			
e.			
f.			
g.			
h.			
i.			
j.			
k.			
l.			

Problem 3-27 (Continued) Name ____________________

2.

Accounts Receivable

Raw Materials

Work in Process

Finished Goods

Manufacturing Overhead

Accounts Payable

Accumulated Depreciation

Depreciation Expense

Salaries & Wages Payable

Salaries Expense

Problem 3-27 (Continued) Name ______________________

Miscellaneous Expense	

Advertising Expense	

Rent Expense	

Cost of Goods Sold	

Sales	

Problem 3-27 (Continued) Name ______________________

3. **SOUTHWORTH COMPANY**
Schedule of Cost of Goods Manufactured

4. Journal entry:

SOUTHWORTH COMPANY
Schedule of Cost of Goods Sold

 Name ______________________

5. SOUTHWORTH COMPANY
Income Statement

6. Total billed price and price per unit:

Case 3-28 Name ______________________

1. Predetermined overhead rate:

Components of Work in Process balance at April 30:

Raw Materials

Work in Process

Finished Goods

Case 3-28 (Continued) **Name** ____________________

Manufacturing Overhead

Accounts Payable

Cost of Goods Sold

Case 3-29 Name ______________________

1. Impact of shaving 5% off the estimated direct-labor hours in the base for the predetermined overhead rate:

2. Recommendation:

Case 3-29 (Continued) **Name** ____________________

2. (continued)

Case 3-30 Name ______________________

1. Under- or overapplied overhead (assuming traditional approach):

TURBO DRIVES, INC.
Income Statement: Traditional Approach

TURBO DRIVES, INC.
Income Statement: New Approach

Case 3-30 (Continued) Name ____________________

2. Under- or overapplied overhead (assuming traditional approach):

TURBO DRIVES, INC.
Income Statement: Traditional Approach

Actual number of units to be produced (under the new approach):

2. (continued)

TURBO DRIVES, INC.
Income Statement: New Approach

3. Impact on net operating income:

Case 3-30 (Continued) Name ______________________________

4. Comments regarding ability to perform "hat trick" under new method:

5. Conclusion as to whether "hat trick" is ethical:

Case 3-31 Name ______________________

1. Revised predetermined overhead rate:

2. Impact of acquisition of automated milling machine:

3. Impact of revision of predetermined overhead rate:

 Name

4. Consequences:

Group Exercise 3-32 **Name** ______________________

Name ____________________

Problem 4-14 Name ______________________

Weighted-Average Method

1. Computation of equivalent units:

		Quantity Schedule	Equivalent Units (EU)		
			Materials	Labor	Overhead

2. Cost reconciliation:

		Total Cost	Equivalent Units (EU)		
			Materials	Labor	Overhead

Problem 4-15 Name ______________________

Weighted-Average Method
Quantity schedule and equivalent units:

		Quantity Schedule	Equivalent Units (EU)	
			Materials	Conversion

Costs per equivalent unit:

		Total	Materials	Conversion	Whole Unit

Cost reconciliation:

		Costs	Equivalent Units (EU)	
			Materials	Conversion

Problem 4-16 Name ____________________

FIFO Method
Quantity schedule and equivalent units:

		Quantity Schedule	Equivalent Units (EU)	
			Materials	Conversion

Costs per equivalent unit:

		Total	Materials	Conversion	Whole Unit

Problem 4-16 (Continued) **Name** ______________________

Cost reconciliation:

		Costs	Equivalent Units (EU) Materials	Conversion

Problem 4-17 Name ____________________

Weighted-Average Method

1. Quantity schedule and equivalent units:

		Quantity Schedule	Equivalent Units (EU)	
			Materials	Conversion

2. Costs per equivalent unit:

		Total Cost	Materials	Conversion	Whole Unit

Problem 4-17 (Continued) Name ____________________

3. Cost reconciliation:

		Total Cost	Equivalent Units (EU) Materials	Equivalent Units (EU) Conversion

Problem 4-18 Name ______________________

FIFO Method

1. Quantity schedule and equivalent units:

		Quantity Schedule	Equivalent Units (EU)	
			Materials	Conversion

2. Costs per equivalent unit:

		Total Cost	Materials	Conversion	Whole Unit

Problem 4-18 (Continued) **Name** ______________________________

3. Cost reconciliation:

		Total Cost	Equivalent Units (EU) Materials	Equivalent Units (EU) Conversion

Problem 4-19 Name ______________________

Weighted-Average Method

1. Units started and completed:

2. Equivalent units:

		Quantity Schedule	Equivalent Units (EU)	
			Materials	Conversion

3. Costs per equivalent unit:

		Total Cost	Materials	Conversion	Whole Unit

4. Ending Work in Process verification:

 Name ______________________

5. Comments on method used to estimate incremental cost:

Problem 4-20 Name ______________________

Weighted-Average Method

1. Quantity schedule and equivalent units:

		Quantity Schedule	Equivalent Units (EU)	
			Materials	Labor & Overhead

Costs per equivalent unit:

		Total	Materials	Labor & Overhead	Whole Unit

Problem 4-20 (Continued) **Name** ____________________

Cost reconciliation:

		Total Cost	Equivalent Units (EU) Materials	Conversion

2. Criticism:

Problem 4-21 Name ______________________________

FIFO Method

1. Quantity schedule and equivalent Units:

		Quantity Schedule	Equivalent Units (EU) Materials	Labor & Overhead

Costs per equivalent unit:

		Total	Materials	Labor & Overhead	Whole Unit

Problem 4-21 (Continued) **Name** ______________________

Cost reconciliation:

		Total Cost	Equivalent Units (EU)	
			Materials	Conversion

Problem 4-22 Name ____________________

Weighted-Average Method

1. Equivalent units:

		Materials	Conversion

Costs per equivalent unit:

		Total Cost	Materials	Conversion	Whole Unit

2. Amount of cost assigned to ending inventory:

		Work in Process	Finished Goods	Total

Problem 4-22 (Continued) **Name** ______________________

3. Necessary adjustments:

		Work in Process	Finished Goods	Total

Entry:

	Debit	Credit

4. Computation of cost of goods sold:

Problem 4-23 **Name** ____________________

Weighted-Average Method

1. Entries:

		Debit	Credit
a.			
b.			
c.			
d.			
e.			
f.			
g.			

Problem 4-23 (Continued) Name ______________________________

3. Posting of entries to T-accounts:

Work in Process— Bottling

Work in Process— Blending

Manufacturing Overhead

Finished Goods

Raw Materials

Accounts Payable

Salaries & Wages Payable

Sales

Accounts Receivable

Cost of Goods Sold

Problem 4-23 (Continued) **Name** ____________________

3. Quantity schedule and equivalent units:

		Quantity Schedule	Equivalent Units (EU)		
			Materials	Labor	Overhead

Problem 4-23 (Continued) **Name** ____________________

2. Costs per equivalent unit:

	Total Cost	Materials	Labor	Overhead	Whole Unit

3. Cost reconciliation:

	Total Cost	Equivalent Units (EU)		
		Materials	Labor	Overhead

Problem 4-24 **Name** ____________________

Weighted-Average Method

1. Entries:

		Debit	Credit
a.			
b.			
c.			
d.			
e.			
f.			
g.			

Problem 4-24 (Continued) Name ______________________

2. Posting of entries to T-accounts:

Raw Materials	

Accounts Receivable	

Work in Process— Assembly	

Work in Process— Testing and Packaging	

Manufacturing Overhead	

Finished Goods	

Salaries & Wages Payable	

Accounts Payable	

Sales	

Cost of Goods Sold	

Problem 4-24 (Continued) **Name** ______________________

3. Quantity schedule and equivalent units:

		Quantity Schedule	Equivalent Units (EU)		
			Materials	Labor	Overhead

Problem 4-24 (Continued) Name ______________________

2. Costs per equivalent unit:

	Total Cost	Materials	Labor	Overhead	Whole Unit

3. Cost reconciliation:

	Total Cost	Equivalent Units (EU)		
		Materials	Labor	Overhead

Case 4-25 Name ____________________

1. Computation of cost of goods sold:

		Transferred In	Conversion	Whole Unit

2. Roseville production manager's desire concerning estimated percentage completion:

Case 4-25 (Continued) Name ____________________

3. Percentage completion figure that would increase net operating income by $62,500:

 Name ____________________

3. Verification:

		Transferred In	Conversion	Whole Unit

4. Decision of Kansas City production manager concerning request to alter estimates of the percentage completion:

Case 4-26 Name ______________________________

Weighted-Average Method
Quantity schedule and equivalent units:

		Quantity Schedule	Equivalent Units (EU) Transferred In	Materials	Conversion

 Name ______________________

Costs per equivalent unit:

		Total Cost	Transferred In	Materials	Conversion	Whole Unit

Cost reconciliation:

			Equivalent Units (EU)		
		Total Cost	Transferred In	Materials	Conversion

2. Why unit cost on report prepared by accountant is so high:

Case 4-27 Name ______________________

FIFO Method

1. Quantity schedule and equivalent units:

		Quantity Schedule	Equivalent Units (EU)		
			Transferred In	Materials	Conversion

Costs per equivalent unit:

		Total Cost	Equivalent Units (EU)		
			Transferred In	Materials	Conversion

Case 4-27 (Continued) **Name** ______________________

Cost reconciliation:

		Total Cost	Transferred In	Materials	Conversion

2. Effects of cost-cutting program under weighted-average method and FIFO method:

Case 4-28

Name

Problem 5-11 Name ____________________

1. Cost behavior:

		Variable	Fixed	Mixed
	Cost of goods sold			
	Shipping expense			
	Advertising expense			
	Salaries and commissions			
	Insurance expense			
	Depreciation expense			

2. Analysis of the mixed expenses:

		Units	Shipping Expense	Salaries and Comm. Expense

Variable cost element:

Shipping expense:

Salaries and commission expense:

Fixed cost element:

		Shipping Expense	Salaries and Comm. Expense

Problem 5-11 (Continued) Name

Cost formulas:

Shipping expense:

Salaries and commission expense:

3.

FRANKEL LTD.
Income Statement
For the Month Ended June 30

Problem 5-12 Name ____________________

1.

HOUSE OF ORGANS, INC.
Income Statement
For the Month Ended November 30

 Name ______________________

2.

HOUSE OF ORGANS, INC.
Income Statement
For the Month Ended November 30

	Total	Per Unit

3. Comments regarding presentation of fixed costs:

Problem 5-13 Name ____________________

1. Estimate of variable cost per league and the total fixed cost per year:

Number of Leagues	Total Cost (Y)

2. Cost formula (linear equation form):

3. Expected total cost for seven leagues:

Problem with using above cost formula to derive total cost figure:

4. Scattergraph:

Problem 5-14 **Name** ____________________

1. Graph identification:

a.

b.

c.

d.

e.

f.

g.

h.

i.

2. Benefits of knowledge of cost behavior when analyzing cost structure:

Problem 5-15 Name ______________________

1. Estimate of maintenance cost:

	Level of Activity	
	40,000 MH	70,000 MH

2. High-low analysis of maintenance cost:

	Maintenance Cost	Machine-Hours

Variable cost element:

Fixed cost element:

Cost formula:

Problem 5-15 (Continued) **Name** ______________________

3. Total overhead costs expressed in linear equation form:

	Variable Rate per Machine-Hour	Fixed Cost

Cost formula:

4. Total overhead costs at an operating activity level of 45,000 machine-hours:

Problem 5-16 Name ____________________

1. Maintenance cost at 80,000 MH level of activity:

	Level of Activity	
	60,000 MH	80,000 MH

2. High-low analysis of maintenance cost:

	Maintenance Cost	Machine-Hours

Variable cost element:

Fixed cost element:

Cost formula:

3. Total expected overhead costs at 65,000 machine-hours:

Problem 5-17 Name ____________________

1. Estimates of amount of manufacturing overhead cost added to production:

	July–Low 9,000 Units	October–High 12,000 Units

2. High-low analysis:

	Units Produced	Cost Observed

Variable cost element:

Fixed cost element:

Cost formula:

Problem 5-17 (Continued) Name ____________________

3. Cost of goods manufactured if 9,500 units are produced:

Problem 5-18 Name ____________________

1. High-Low Method:

	Number of Ingots	Power Cost

Variable cost element:

Fixed cost element:

Cost formula:

2. Scattergraph method (see scattergraph on following page):

Problem 5-18 (Continued) Name ____________________

2. (Continued) Scattergraph:

Problem 5-19

Name ______________________________

1. Least squares regression method:

Number of Ingots	Power Cost

Problem 5-19 (Continued) **Name** ____________________

2. Comparison of results using the three methods:

	Method	Total Fixed Cost	Variable Cost per Ingot
	High-low		
	Quick-and-dirty scattergraph		
	Least squares		

Comments on accuracy and usefulness of data derived by each method:

Problem 5-20 **Name** ______________________

1. Scattergraph:

Problem 5-20 (Continued) Name

2. Conclusion regarding correctness of President's assumptions:

Approximate total fixed cost:

Approximate variable cost per meal served:

Problem 5-21 **Name** ______________________

1. Least squares regression method:

Meals Served (000s) (X)	Total Cost (Y)

2. Cost formula:

Problem 5-22 Name ____________________

1. Least squares regression method:

Units Sold (000) (X)	Shipping Expense (Y)

Problem 5-22 (Continued) Name ______________________

2.

ALDEN COMPANY
Budgeted Income Statement
For the First Quarter of Year 3

Case 5-23 Name

1. Contribution to profit of a standard 120-guest cocktail party at $45 per guest:

Name ____________________

Case 5-23 (Continued) Name ______________________

2. Amount that should be bid for the charity event (in terms of price per guest):

3. Recommendation regarding a bid below normal $45 per guest:

Case 5-24 **Name** ____________________

1. Predetermined overhead rate (direct labor-hours allocation base):

Predetermined overhead rate (machine-hours allocation base):

2. Electrical cost for custom tool job using direct labor-hours:

Electrical cost for custom tool job using machine-hours:

3. Scattergraph for electrical costs and machine-hours:

Case 5-24 (Continued) Name ______________________

3. (continued) Scattergraph for electrical costs and direct labor-hours:

Comments:

Case 5-24 (Continued) Name ______________________

4. Lease squares regression method:

Machine Hours (X)	Electrical Costs (Y)

Cost formula:

5. Amount of electrical cost actually caused by the custom job for the watchmaker:

Case 5-24 (Continued) **Name** ______________________

6. Factors that are likely to affect consumption of electrical power:

Case 5-25 Name ____________________

1. Scattergraph (units produced as activity base):

2. Scattergraph (number of workdays as activity base):

Case 5-25 (Continued) Name ______________

3. Recommendation regarding the measure of activity that should be used as the activity base for explaining janitorial labor cost:

Case 5-26 **Name** ______________________

1. a. Least squares regression method:

Tons Mined (000s) (X)	Utilities Cost (Y)

Cost formula:

b. Scattergraph (utility costs versus tons mined):

Case 5-26 (Continued) Name ______________________

2. a. Lease squares regression method:

DLHs (000) (X)	Utilities Cost (Y)

Cost formula:

b. Scattergraph (utility costs versus direct labor-hours):

Case 5-26 (Continued) Name ____________________

3. Recommendation:

Group Exercise 5-27

Name ______________________________

Group Exercise 5-27 (Continued)   Name ______________________

Problem 6-9 Name ______________________

1. Contribution margin (CM) ratio:

		Total	Per Unit	%

Break-even point (in units and dollars):

2. Incremental contribution margin:

3. Income statement (if changes are adopted):

4. Target profit analysis:

Problem 6-9 (Continued) **Name** ______________________

5. a. New CM ratio:

		Per Unit	%

New break-even point (in units and dollars):

b. Comparative income statements:

	Not Automated			Automated		
	Total	Per Unit	%	Total	Per Unit	%

c. Recommendation:

Problem 6-10 Name ______________________

1. Annual break-even point (in dollars and units):

2. Graph paper for preparing the CVP graph has been provided on the following page.

3. Net operating income (loss) if 19,000 units are sold:

4. New break-even point (in dollars and units):

5. Calculation of new net operating income (loss):

Problem 6-10 (Continued) Name ______________________

2. Cost-volume-profit graph:

Problem 6-10 (Continued) Name ______________________

6. a. New break-even point (in dollars and units):

b. Recommendation:

Problem 6-11 **Name** ______________________________

1. Contribution income statement:

	Product			
	Sinks	Vanities	Mirrors	Total

2. Break-even point (in dollars):

3. Memo to the President:

Problem 6-12 Name ______________________

1. CM ratio:

2. Break-even point (in dollars) using CM ratio:

3. Increase in net operating income if sales increase by $45,000:

4. a. Degree of operating leverage (at current level of sales):

b. Increase in net operating income if sales increase by 15%:

5. Comparative income statements:

	Last Year: 28,000 units		Proposed: 42,000 units	
	Amount	Per Unit	Amount	Per Unit

Recommendation:

Problem 6-12 (Continued) **Name** ______________________

6. Amount by which advertising can be increased with net operating income remaining unchanged:

Problem 6-13 **Name** ______________________

1. Net operating income (loss):

2. Break-even point (in units and Swiss franc sales):

3. Maximum profit that can be earned:

Unit Sales Price	Unit Variable Expense	Unit Contribution Margin	Volume (Units)	Total Contribution Margin	Fixed Expenses	Net Operating Income

4. New break-even point (in units and Swiss franc sales):

Problem 6-14 Name ______________________

1. Monthly break-even point (in units and dollars):

Problem 6-14 (Continued) Name

2. Target profit analysis:

3. New target profit analysis:

Problem 6-15 Name ______________________

1. (1)
   (2)
   (3)
   (4)
   (5)
   (6)
   (7)
   (8)
   (9)

2. a.

   b.

   c.

   d.

   e.

   f.

   g.

   h.

Problem 6-16 Name ______________________

1. Target profit analysis:

2. Break-even point (in units and dollars):

Problem 6-17 Name ____________________

1. a. Contribution income statement:

	Alvaro		Bazan		Total	
	Pesetas	%	Pesetas	%	Pesetas	%

b. Break-even point (in pesetas) and margin of safety:

 Name ____________________

2. a. Contribution income statement:

	Alvaro		Bazan		Cano		Total	
	Pesetas	%	Pesetas	%	Pesetas	%	Pesetas	%

b. New break-even point (in pesetas) and margin of safety:

Problem 6-18 Name ______________________

1. a. CM ratio and break-even point (in units):

b. Degree of operating leverage at last year's level of sales:

2. New CM ratio and new break-even point (in units):

3. Target profit analysis:

Problem 6-18 (Continued) **Name** ______________________

4. New selling price:

5. New CM ratio and new break-even point (in units):

6. a. Target profit analysis:

Problem 6-18 (Continued)   Name ______________________

b. Contribution income statement:

Degree of operating leverage:

c. Conclusion regarding construction of new plant:

Problem 6-19 **Name** ____________________

1. Break-even point (in units and dollars):

2. Cost-volume-profit graph:

Problem 6-19 (Continued) **Name** ______________________________

3. Target profit analysis:

4. Incremental approach:

Conclusion:

5. a. Degree of operating leverage:

b. Expected percentage increase in net operating income:

Problem 6-20 Name ______________________

1. Comparative income statements:

	Present			Proposed		
	Amount	Per Unit	%	Amount	Per Unit	%

2.	Present	Proposed
a. Degree of operating leverage:		
b. Break-even point (in dollars):		
c. Margin of safety:		

3. Factor paramount in deciding whether to purchase the new equipment:

Problem 6-20 (Continued) **Name** ______________________

4. Break-even point (in dollars):

Risks in president's proposal:

Problem 6-21 **Name** ______________________________

1. April's income statement:

	Standard	%	Deluxe	%	Pro	%	Total	%

Problem 6-21 (Continued) **Name** ______________________

May's income statement:

	Standard	%	Deluxe	%	Pro	%	Total	%

2. Explanation:

3. Break-even point (in dollars):

4. Explanation of change in break-even point from April to May:

5. Incremental analysis:

Case 6-22 Name ______________________

1. and 2. Income statement in contribution format:

	Part 1		Part 2a		Part 2b	
	Total	Per Unit	Total	Per Unit	Total	Per Unit

Case 6-22 (Continued) Name ______________________

3. Target profit analysis:

4. Increase in advertising that will maintain target return:

5. Quoted price per unit:

Case 6-23 Name ____________________

1. Break-even point (in dollars) using CM ratio:

	Frog	Minnow	Worm	Total

2. a. Break-even point (in units) using contribution margin approach:

	Frog	Minnow	Worm

b. Overall profit to company if company sells the break-even quantities:

b. (continued)

	Frog	Minnow	Worm	Total

Case 6-23 (Continued) Name ____________________

 Name

Case 6-24 Name ____________________

1. Total annual fixed cost of Cardiac Care Department:

Annual Patient-Days	Aides @ $18,000	Nurses @ $29,000	Supervising Nurses @ $38,000	Total Personnel	Other Fixed Costs	Total Fixed Cost

2. Break-even point for each range of activity:

Annual Patient-Days	Total Fixed Cost	Contribution Margin	Break-Even	Within Relevant Range?

Name ______________________

3. Level of activity required to earn profit of $360,000:

Annual Patient-Days	Total Fixed Cost	Target Profit	Total Fixed Cost + Target Profit	Contribution Margin	Ability to Attain Target Profit	Within Relevant Range?

Case 6-25 Name ____________________

1. Contribution format income statement for the three alternatives:

	18% Commission	20% Commission	Own Sales Force

Case 6-25 (Continued) Name ______________________

2. a. Break-even points (in dollars) if commission rate is unchanged at 18%:

b. Break-even point (in dollars) if commission rate increases to 20%:

c. Break-even point (in dollars) if company employs own sales force:

3. Target profit analysis:

4. Volume of sales at which net income is equal regardless of decision:

 Name ____________________

5. Graph showing both alternatives:

6. Memorandum:

Case 6-25 (Continued) Name

6. (continued)

Case 6-26 Name ____________________

1. a.

PUTREX COMPANY
Actual Income Statement
For the Month Ended July 31

	Total	Per Unit	%

Supporting calculations:

1. b. Break-even point (in units and dollars):

c. Margin of safety (in dollars and percentage):

d. Degree of operating leverage:

2. a.

PUTREX COMPANY
Projected Income Statement
For the Month Ended August 31

	Total	Per Unit	%

Case 6-26 (Continued) Name

2. b. Margin of safety:

Degree of operating leverage:

3. Target profit analysis:

Group Exercise 6-27 **Name** ______________________

Name ______________________________

Group Exercise 6-28 Name ____________________

1, 2, and 3.

	Affected by adding service to an airport?	Affected by adding a flight?	Variable with respect to seats-filled?
Fuel and oil			
Flying operations labor (flight crews—pilots, copilots, navigators, and flight engineers)			
Passenger service labor (flight attendants)			
Aircraft traffic and serving labor (personnel servicing aircraft and handling passengers at gates, baggage, and cargo)			
Promotions and sales labor (reservations and sales agents, advertising and publicity)			
Maintenance labor (maintenance of flight equipment and ground property and equipment)			
Maintenance materials and overhead			
Ground property and equipment (landing fees, and rental expenses and depreciation for ground property and equipment)			
Flight equipment (rental expenses and depreciation on aircraft frames and engines)			
General overhead (administrative personnel, utilities, insurance, communications, etc.)			

 Name ____________________

4.

Group Exercise 6-29 Name ______________________

1. Cost of four year's tuition at a private college in ten years and affordability:

2. Cost of adding extra student to a typical class and explanation:

3. Impact of increasing enrollment and economies of scale on costs and tuition:

4. Colleges (public or private) that will be helped most by increasing enrollment:

Problem 7-8 Name ____________________

1. Unit product cost under variable costing approach:

Variable costing income statements:

	Year 1	Year 2

2. Reconciliation of absorption costing and variable costing net operating income figures:

	Year 1	Year 2

Problem 7-9 **Name** ______________________

1. a. Unit product cost under absorption costing:

b. Absorption costing income statement:

2. a. Unit product cost under variable costing:

Problem 7-9 (Continued) Name ____________________

b. Variable costing income statement:

3. Reason for any different on reported net operating income:

Impact of difference on reported net operating income:

Problem 7-10 **Name** ____________________

1. a. and b. Unit product cost:

	Absorption Costing	Variable Costing

2. Income statement using absorption costing:

Problem 7-10 (Continued) **Name** ______________________

3. Income statement using variable costing:

4. Statement preferred when negotiating with bank:

5. Reconciliation of absorption costing and variable costing net operating income figures:

Problem 7-11 Name ______________________

1. a. and b. Unit product cost:

	Absorption Costing	Variable Costing

2. Income statement using contribution approach with variable costing:

	May	June

3. Reconciliation of variable costing and absorption costing net operating income:

	May	June

4. Explanation of May income statement:

5. Reconciliation of absorption costing and variable costing operating income:

Problem 7-12 Name ______________________

1. a. Unit product cost under absorption costing:

b. Income statement for first month of operations using absorption costing:

c. Reconciliation of variable costing and absorption costing net operating income:

Problem 7-12 (Continued) **Name** ______________________

2. Comments regarding CPA's suggestion that company really earned a "profit" for the month:

3. a. Income statement for second month of operations using variable costing:

Problem 7-12 (Continued) Name ____________________

b. Income statement for second month of operations using absorption costing:

c. Reconciliation of variable costing and absorption costing net operating income:

Problem 7-13 Name ____________________

1. Income statements using contribution approach with variable costing:

	Year 1	Year 2	Year 3

2. a. Unit product costing under absorption costing:

	Year 1	Year 2	Year 3

b. Reconciliation of variable costing and absorption costing net operating income:

	Year 1	Year 2	Year 3

Problem 7-13 (Continued) Name

3. Explanation for higher net operating income in Year 2 even though fewer units were sold:

4. Explanation for loss in Year 3 and profit in Year 1 even though same number of units were sold:

Problem 7-13 (Continued) Name ______________________

5. a. Impact on operations in Year 2 and Year 3 if JIT inventory methods were used:

b. Impact on net operating income in Year 2 and Year 3 if JIT had been in use and explanation for any differences between these income figures and those reported by the company:

Income statements under absorption costing (if JIT in use during Years 2 and 3):

	Year 1	Year 2	Year 3

Problem 7-14 Name ______________________

1. Units that should be scheduled for production (assuming variable costing):

Impact on division's reported profit for the year:

2. Units that should be scheduled for production (assuming absorption costing):

Problem 7-14 (Continued) **Name** ______________________

3. Ethical issues involved in decision Mr. Constantinos must make:

Problem 7-15 Name ____________________

1. a. and b. Unit product cost:

	Absorption Costing		Variable Costing	
	Year 1	Year 2	Year 1	Year 2

2. Income statements using contribution approach under variable costing:

	Year 1		Year 2	

3. Reconciliation of variable costing and absorption costing net operating income:

	Year 1	Year 2

Problem 7-15 (Continued) Name ______________________

4. Explanation for higher net operating income in Year 2 than in Year 1 even though the same number of units were sold:

5. a. Impact on operations in Year 2 if company had been using JIT and inventories had been eliminated:

b. Net operating income under absorption costing if JIT had been in use in Year 2 and ending inventories were zero and explanation for difference between this figure and that reported by company:

Case 7-16 **Name** ______________________

1. Units to be sold to meet the target net operating income of $4,800,000:

2. Unit product cost (at a production level of 210,000 units):

Revised budgeted income statement:

3. Units to be produced to show a profit of at least $4,800,000 under absorption costing:

Case 7-16 (Continued) Name ______________________

4. Unit product cost (at production level determined in part 3 above):

Income statement using absorption costing method:

5. Recommendation regarding plan to build ending inventories in order to attain the target profit:

 Name ______________________

5. (Continued)

6. Advice regarding determination of bonuses in the future:

Case 7-17 **Name** ____________________

1. Income statements using contribution approach with variable costing:

	April	May	June

Case 7-17 (Continued) Name

2. Monthly break-even point in units under variable costing:

3. Explanation regarding erratic nature of profits and lack of correlation with changes in sales volume:

 Name ______________________

4. Schedule showing inventories, production, and sales in units:

	Beginning Inventory	Units Produced	Units Sold	Ending Inventory
April				
May				
June				

Calculation of fixed manufacturing overhead rate per unit of product:

Reconciliation of variable costing and absorption costing net operating income (loss):

	April	May	June

5. a. Units produced during June under JIT:

b. Expectation regarding difference between net operating income reported under absorption costing and under variable costing in next quarter:

c. Hot JIT would help break-even analysis "make sense" under absorption costing:

Case 7-18 Name ______________________

1. Characteristic of absorption costing that caused drop in net operating income for the second quarter and explanation:

2. Income statements using contribution approach under variable costing:

	First Quarter	Second Quarter

Case 7-18 (Continued) Name ______________________

3. Reconciliation of absorption costing and variable costing net operating income:

	First Quarter	Second Quarter

4. Advantages and disadvantages of using variable costing for internal reporting:

5. a. Units that would have been produced during second quarter under JIT:

Income statement for second quarter assuming move to JIT (not required):

b.

Group Exercise 7-19 Name ____________________

1. Basis for inventory valuation and cost of goods sold determination for external reporting purposes:

2. Explanation of concept of "phantom" or "illusory" profits:

3. Conclusion regarding such "fictitious" profits and conditions that might otherwise cause increased profits:

4. Conditions that might otherwise cause decreased profits:

Group Exercise 7-20 Name ______________________

1. Implications of trend toward higher proportions of overhead for arguments favoring absorption costing:

Implications for arguments favoring variable costing:

2. Impact of inventory buildups or inventory liquidations on future reporting earnings compared with past reported earnings (assuming absorption costing):

3. Top management's preference for basing its evaluations on variable costing or on full absorption costing:

Problem 8-13 Name ______________________

1. a. Predetermined overhead rate:

b. Unit costs

	Model	
	XR7	ZD5

2. a. Activity rates (predetermined overhead rates) for activity cost pools:

Activity Cost Pool	Total Cost	Total Activity	Activity Rate
Machine setups			
Special milling			
General factory			

Amount of overhead cost that would be applied to each product:

		Model	
		XR7	ZD5

Problem 8-13 (Continued) Name ____________________

b. Overhead costs expressed on a per unit basis:

	Model	
	XR7	ZD5

Unit product cost of each model under activity-based costing:

	Model	
	XR7	ZD5

3.

Problem 8-14 Name ____________________

1. First-stage allocation of costs to the activity cost pools:

Costs	Job Size	Estimating and Job Setup	Working on Nonroutine Jobs	Other	Totals
Wages and salaries					
Disposal fees					
Equipment depreciation					
On-site supplies					
Office expenses					
Licensing and insurance					
Total cost					

2. Activity rates for the activity cost pools:

Activity Cost Pool	Total Cost	Total Activity	Activity Rate
Job size			
Estimating and job setup			
Working on nonroutine jobs			

3. a. Total cost and average cost per thousand square feet – routine 2,000-square-foot asbestos removal job:

b. Total cost and average cost per thousand square feet – routine 4,000-square-foot asbestos removal job:

 Name ______________________

c. Total cost and average cost per thousand square feet – nonroutine 2,000-square-foot asbestos removal job:

4. Comments regarding adequacy of present policy for bidding on jobs:

Problem 8-15 Name

1. Cost of local commercials market:

Activity Cost Pool	Activity Rate	Activity	ABC Cost
Animation concept			
Animation production			
Contract administration			

2. Product margin of local commercials market:

3. Recommendation concerning local commercials market:

Problem 8-16

Name ____________________

1. Detailed cost analysis of the local commercial market:

	Activity Rates		
	Animation Concept	Animation Production	Contract Admin.
Technical staff salaries			
Animation equipment depreciation			
Administrative wages and salaries			
Supplies costs			
Facility costs			
Total			

	Animation Concepts	Animation Production	Contract Admin.	Total
Activity level				
Technical staff salaries				
Animation equipment depreciation				
Administrative wages and salaries				
Supplies costs				
Facility costs				
Total				

Problem 8-16 **Name** ____________________

2. Action analysis report:

3. Recommendation concerning local commercials market:

Problem 8-17 **Name** ______________________

1. Predetermined overhead rate (using direct labor-hours as base):

Unit product cost of each model:

	Deluxe	Regular

2. Predetermined overhead rates (activity rates) for the four activity cost pools:

Activity Cost Pool	Estimated Overhead Cost	Expected Activity	Predetermined Overhead Rate
Purchase orders			
Scrap rework orders			
Product testing			
Machine related			

3. Overhead applied to each product:

The Deluxe Model

Activity Cost Pool	Predetermined Overhead Rate	Activity	Overhead Applied

The Regular Model

Activity Cost Pool	Predetermined Overhead Rate	Activity	Overhead Applied

Problem 8-17 (Continued) **Name** ______________________

b. Unit product cost of each model using activity-based costing system:

		Deluxe	Regular

4.

Problem 8-18 Name ______________________

1. First-stage allocation of costs to activity cost pools:

	Meal Preparation	Flight-related	Customer Service	Other	Totals
Cooks and delivery personnel wages					
Kitchen supplies					
Chef salaries					
Equipment depreciation					
Administrative salaries and wages					
Building costs					
Total costs					

2. Activity rates at the CDG operation:

	Meal Preparation	Flight-related	Customer Service
Cooks and delivery personnel wages			
Kitchen supplies			
Chef salaries			
Equipment depreciation			
Administrative salaries and wages			
Building costs			
Total costs			

3. Suggestions for top management of Chefs de Vitesse SA:

Problem 8-19 Name ______________________

1. First-stage allocation of costs to activity cost pools:

	Distribution of Resource Consumption Across Activity Cost Pools				
	Cleaning Carpets	Travel to Jobs	Job Support	Other	Total
Wages					
Cleaning supplies					
Cleaning equipment (depreciation)					
Vehicle expenses					
Office expenses					
President's compensation					

	Cleaning Carpets	Travel to Jobs	Job Support	Other	Total
Wages					
Cleaning supplies					
Cleaning equipment (depreciation)					
Vehicle expenses					
Office expenses					
President's compensation					

2. Activity rates:

Activity Cost Pool	Total Cost	Total Activity	Activity Rate
Cleaning carpets			
Travel to jobs			
Job support			
Total			

Problem 8-19 (Continued) **Name** ______________________

3. Cost for Lazy Bee Ranch job:

Activity Cost Pool	Activity Rate	Activity	ABC Cost
Cleaning carpets			
Travel to jobs			
Job support			
Total			

4. Product margin from Lazy Bee Ranch job:

5.

Problem 8-19 (Continued) **Name** ______________________

6.

Problem 8-20

Name ______________________

1. First-stage allocation of costs to activity cost pools:

	Distribution of Resource Consumption Across Activity Pools				
	Cleaning Carpets	Travel to Jobs	Job Support	Other	Totals
Wages	%	%	%	%	100%
Cleaning supplies	%	%	%	%	100%
Cleaning equipment depreciation	%	%	%	%	100%
Vehicle expenses	%	%	%	%	100%
Office expenses	%	%	%	%	100%
President's compensation	%	%	%	%	100%

	Cleaning Carpets	Travel to Jobs	Job Support	Other	Totals
Wages					
Cleaning supplies					
Cleaning equipment depreciation					
Vehicle expenses					
Office expenses					
President's compensation					

Problem 8-20 (Continued) Name ______________________

2. Activity rates:

	Cleaning Carpets	Travel to Jobs	Job Support
Total activity			
Wages			
Cleaning supplies			
Cleaning equipment depreciation			
Vehicle expenses			
Office expenses			
President's compensation			
Total costs			

3. Cost for the Lazy Blue Ranch job:

	Cleaning Carpets	Travel to Jobs	Job Support	Total
Activity for the Lazy Boy job				
Wages				
Cleaning supplies				
Cleaning equipment depreciation				
Vehicle expenses				
Office expenses				
President's compensation				
Total costs				

Problem 8-20 (Continued) Name ______________________

4. Action analysis report:

3. Conclusion about profitability of Lazy Bee Ranch job:

6. Advice to president concerning pricing jobs in the future:

Problem 8-21 **Name** ____________________

1. Predetermined overhead rate (using direct labor-hours as base):

2. Predetermined overhead rates for the four activity cost pools:

Activity Center	Estimated Overhead Costs	Expected Activity	Predetermined Overhead Rate
Maintaining parts inventory			
Processing purchase orders			
Quality control			
Machine-related			

Problem 8-21 (Continued) Name ______________________

3. a. Total amount of overhead cost applied to each product and overhead cost per unit of each product using activity-based costing:

	Mono-circuit		Bi-circuit	
	Expected Activity	Amount	Expected Activity	Amount

b. Unit product costs (using activity-based costing):

	Mono-circuit	Bi-circuit

4.

Case 8-22 **Name** ______________________

1.

Activity Cost Pool	Estimated Overhead Cost	Expected Activity	Activity Rate

Calculations:

Overhead cost charged to each product:

		Standard		Specialty	
		Activity	Amount	Activity	Amount

Overhead cost per unit of product:

2. Unit product costs using activity-based costing (with conventional costing product costs for comparison):

	Activity-Based Costing		Direct Labor-Hour Base	
	Standard	Specialty	Standard	Specialty

3. Evaluation of concern about profitability of the two product lines and recommendation:

 Name ______________________

4. Comments about competition's inability to touch FirstLine's price on specialty business:

Case 8-23 Name ____________

1. a. Predetermined overhead rate (using traditional approach):

b. Total margin for windows ordered (using traditional costing system):

	Avon Construction	Lynx Builders

2. a. First-stage allocation of costs to the activity pools:

	Making Windows	Processing Orders	Customer Relations	Other	Totals
Indirect factory wages					
Production equipment depreciation					
Other factory costs					
Administrative wages and salaries					
Office expenses					
Marketing expenses					
Total cost					

Case 8-23 (Continued) Name ____________________

b. Activity rates:

	Making Windows	Processing Orders	Customer Relations
Total activity			
Indirect factory wages			
Production equipment depreciation			
Other factory costs			
Administrative wages and salaries			
Office expenses			
Marketing expenses			
Total cost			

c. Overhead cost of serving Avon Construction:

	Making Windows	Processing Orders	Customer Relations	Total
Activity for Avon Construction				
Indirect factory wages				
Production equipment depreciation				
Other factory costs				
Administrative wages and salaries				
Office expenses				
Marketing expenses				
Total cost				

	Making Windows	Processing Orders	Customer Relations	Total
Activity for Lynx Builders				
Indirect factory wages				
Production equipment depreciation				
Other factory costs				
Administrative wages and salaries				
Office expenses				
Marketing expenses				
Total cost				

Case 8-23 (Continued) Name ____________________

d. Action Analysis – Avon Construction

d. Action Analysis – Lynx Builders

Case 8-23 (Continued)　　　　　　Name ____________________

3. Comments regarding profitability and costing systems:

Case 8-24 **Name** ____________________

1. a. Predetermined overhead rate:

b. Unit cost per pound:

	Mona Loa	Malaysian

c. Selling price per pound of coffee:

	Mona Loa	Malaysian

2. a. Overhead rates by activity center:

	Estimated Overhead Costs	Expected Activity	Predetermined Overhead Rate
Purchasing			
Material handling			
Quality control			
Roasting			
Blending			
Packaging			

Case 8-24 (Continued) Name ____________________

Activity for each of the products in the six activity centers:

Number of purchase orders:

Mona Loa

Malaysian

Number of batches:

Mona Loa

Malaysian

Number of setups:

Mona Loa

Malaysian

Roasting hours:

Mona Loa

Malaysian

Blending hours:

Mona Loa

Malaysian

Packaging hours:

Mona Loa

Malaysian

Total amount of manufacturing overhead costs assigned to products:

	Mona Loa		Malaysian	
	Expected Activity	Amount	Expected Activity	Amount
Total overhead cost				

Case 8-24 (Continued) Name ____________

b. Manufacturing overhead cost per pound:

	Mona Loa	Malaysian

c. Unit product costs:

	Mona Loa	Malaysian

3. Memo to the president:

Case 8-25 Name ______________________

1. Predetermined overhead rate (using direct labor-hours as base):

2. Unit product costs:

	B-10	C-20

3. Overhead rates for the activities:

Activity	Estimated Overhead Costs	Expected Activity	Predetermined Manufacturing Overhead Rate
Machine setups			
Quality control			
Purchase orders			
Soldering			
Shipments			
Machine related			

Case 8-25 (Continued) Name ________________

Overhead cost assigned to each product:

	B-10		C-20	
Activity	Expected Activity	Amount	Expected Activity	Amount
Machine setups				
Quality control				
Purchase orders				
Soldering				
Shipments				
Machine related				
Total overhead cost				
Number of units produced				
Overhead cost per unit				

Unit product cost under activity-based costing (with unit product cost under old traditional costing system for comparison):

	Activity-Based Costing		Direct Labor-Hours Base	
	B-10	C-20	B-10	C-20

 Name

Position on recommendation to expand sales of the C-20:

4.

5.

Group Exercise 8-26 **Name** ______________________

1.

2.

Group Exercise 8-27

Name ______________________

1. ______________________

2. ______________________

3. ______________________

Group Exercise 8-28 Name

Problem 9-8 Name ____________________

1. How budgeting system differs from recommended practice:

2. Behavioral implications:

Problem 9-9 Name ____________________

1. Expected cash collections for September:

2. Expected cash disbursements during September for inventory purchases:

3.

CALGON PRODUCTS
Cash Budget
For the Month of September

Problem 9-10 Name ____________________

1. Production budget:

	July	August	September	October

2.

Raw Materials purchases budget:

	July	August	September	Third Quarter

Problem 9-11 Name ____________________

1.

PRISTON COMPANY
Direct Materials Budget

	1st Quarter	2nd Quarter	3rd Quarter	4th Quarter	Year

PRISTON COMPANY
Schedule of Expected Cash Disbursements for Materials

	1st Quarter	2nd Quarter	3rd Quarter	4th Quarter	Year

2.

PRISTON COMPANY
Direct Labor Budget

	1st Quarter	2nd Quarter	3rd Quarter	4th Quarter	Year

Problem 9-12 **Name** ______________________

1.

HARVETON CORPORATION
Direct Labor Budget

	1st Quarter	2nd Quarter	3rd Quarter	4th Quarter	Year

2.

HARVETON CORPORATION
Manufacturing Overhead Budget

	1st Quarter	2nd Quarter	3rd Quarter	4th Quarter	Year

Problem 9-13 Name ____________________

1. Schedule of cash receipts:

Schedule of cash payments for purchases:

PHOTOTEC, INC.
Cash Budget
For the Month of June

 Name ______________________

2.

PHOTOTEC, INC.
Budgeted Income Statement
For the Month of June

3.

PHOTOTEC, INC.
Budgeted Balance Sheet
June 30

Problem 9-14 Name ____________________

1. Schedule of expected cash collections:

	Month			
	April	May	June	Quarter

2. Cash budget:

	Month			
	April	May	June	Quarter

Problem 9-14 (Continued) **Name** ______________________

3. Comments regarding repayment of loan:

Problem 9-15 Name ____________________

1. Comments regarding Stokes' use of budgets as a planning and control tool:

2. Behavioral consequences:

Problem 9-15 (Continued) Name ____________________

3. Recommendation:

Problem 9-16 Name ______________________

1. Sales budget for third quarter:

	Month			
	July	August	September	Quarter

Schedule of expected cash collections from sales:

	Month			
	July	August	September	Quarter

2. Production budget for July through October:

	July	August	September	October

Problem 9-16 (Continued) Name ____________________

3. Material purchases budget for third quarter:

	Month			Quarter
	July	August	September	

Schedule of expected cash disbursements:

	Month			Quarter
	July	August	September	

Problem 9-17 Name ______________________

1. Collections on sales:

	Month			Quarter
	July	August	September	

2. a. Inventory purchases budget:

	July	August	September	October

b. Schedule of expected cash disbursements for inventory:

	Month			Quarter
	July	August	September	

Problem 9-17 (Continued) **Name** ____________________

3.

JANUS PRODUCTS, INC.
Cash Budget
For the Quarter Ended September 30

	Month			
	July	August	September	Quarter

Problem 9-18 Name ______________________

1. a. Schedule of expected cash collections for Year 2:

	Year 2 Quarter				
	First	Second	Third	Fourth	Total

b. Schedule of budgeted cash disbursements for merchandise purchases for Year 2:

	Year 2 Quarter				
	First	Second	Third	Fourth	Total

Problem 9-18 (Continued) **Name** ______________________

2. Expected cash disbursements for operating expenses for Year 2:

	Year 2 Quarter				
	First	Second	Third	Fourth	Total

3. Cash budget for Year 2:

	Year 2 Quarter				
	First	Second	Third	Fourth	Total

Problem 9-19 Name ____________________

1. Schedule of expected cash collections:

	April	May	June	Quarter

2. a. Inventory purchases budget:

	April	May	June	Quarter

b. Schedule of cash disbursement for purchases:

	April	May	June	Quarter

3. Schedule of cash disbursements for operating expenses:

	April	May	June	Quarter

Problem 9-19 (Continued)   Name ______________________

4. Cash budget

	April	May	June	Quarter

5.

NORDIC COMPANY
Income Statement
For the Quarter Ended June 30

 Name ____________

6.

NORDIC COMPANY
Balance Sheet
June 30

Problem 9-20 **Name** ______________________

1. Schedule of expected cash collections:

	January	February	March	Quarter

2. Inventory purchases budget:

	January	February	March	Quarter

Schedule of expected cash disbursements—purchases:

	January	February	March	Quarter

3. Schedule of expected cash disbursements—operating expenses:

	January	February	March	Quarter

Problem 9-20 (Continued) Name ______________________

4. Cash budget:

	January	February	March	Quarter

5.

PICANUY CORPORATION
Income Statement
For the Quarter Ended March 31

Problem 9-20 (Continued)   Name ______________________

6.

PICANUY CORPORATION
Balance Sheet
March 31

Problem 9-21 **Name** ______________________

1. Production budget:

	April	May	June	Quarter

2. Direct materials purchases budget:

	April	May	June	Quarter
Material #208:				
Material #311:				

Problem 9-21 (Continued)   Name ____________________

3. Direct labor budget:

	Units Produced	Direct Labor Hours		Cost per DLH	Total Cost
		Per Unit	Total		

4. Manufacturing overhead budget:

Problem 9-22 **Name** ____________________

1. Collection pattern:

	Percentage of Sales Uncollected at April 30	Percentage to be Collected in May
	%	%
	%	%
	%	%
	%	%

Schedule of expected cash collections:

Problem 9-22 (Continued)　　　Name ______________________

2.

HOUSEHALL COMPANY, LTD.
Cash Budget
May

3.

Case 9-23 **Name** ______________________

1.

a.

b.

c.

d.

2. ____

a. ____

b. ____

c. ____

Case 9-24 **Name** ______________________

1. Cash payments for skate purchases from the manufacturers:

	February	March	April	May	June	July

Payments for purchases:

	February	March	April	May	June	July

Case 9-24 (Continued) Name ______________________

Operating expenses:

	February	March	April	May	June	July

Cash receipts from sales:

	February	March	April	May	June	July

Case 9-24 (Continued) Name ______________________

Cash budget:

	April	May	June	Quarter

2. Importance of cash budgeting:

Case 9-25 Name ____________________

1. a. Sales budget:

	April	May	June	Quarter

b. Schedule of expected cash collections:

	April	May	June	Quarter

c. Budgeted purchases:

	April	May	June	Quarter

d. Budgeted cash disbursements for purchases:

	April	May	June	Quarter

Case 9-25 (Continued) Name ______________________

CRAVAT SALES COMPANY
Cash Budget
For the Three Months Ending June 30

	April	May	June	Quarter

Case 9-25 (Continued) Name ____________________

3.

CRAVAT SALES COMPANY
Budgeted Income Statement
For the Three Months Ended June 30

4.

CRAVAT SALES COMPANY
Budgeted Balance Sheet
June 30

Group Exercise 9-26 Name ______________________

1. ______________________

2. ______________________

3. ______________________

4. ______________________

Problem 10-10 Name ______________________

1. a. Materials price and quantity variances:

(AQ x AP) Actual Quantity of Input, at Actual Price	(AQ x SP) Actual Quantity of Input, at Standard Price	(SQ x SP) Standard Quantity Allowed for Output, at Standard Price

b. Recommendation: ______________________

2. a. Labor rate and efficiency variances:

(AH x AR) Actual Hours of Input, at Actual Rate	(AH x SR) Actual Hours of Input, at Standard Rate	(SH x SR) Standard Hours Allowed for Output, at Standard Rate

b. Recommendation: ______________________

Problem 10-10 (Continued) Name ______________________

3. Variable overhead and spending variances:

(AH x AR) Actual Hours of Input, at Actual Rate	(AH x SR) Actual Hours of Input, at Standard Rate	(SH x SR) Standard Hours Allowed for Output, at Standard Rate

Relation between this efficiency variance and labor efficiency variance:

Problem 10-11 Name ____________________

1. Standard quantity for plates:

Materials price and quantity variances:

(AQ x AP) Actual Quantity of Input, at Actual Price	(AQ x SP) Actual Quantity of Input, at Standard Price	(SQ x SP) Standard Quantity Allowed for Output, at Standard Price

2. a. Standard hours allowed for tests performed during the month:

Labor rate and labor efficiency variances:

(AH x AR) Actual Hours of Input, at Actual Rate	(AH x SR) Actual Hours of Input, at Standard Rate	(SH x SR) Standard Hours Allowed for Output, at Standard Rate

Problem 10-11 (Continued) Name ____________________

b. Recommendation:

3. Variable overhead spending and efficiency variances:

(AH x AR) Actual Hours of Input, at Actual Rate	(AH x SR) Actual Hours of Input, at Standard Rate	(SH x SR) Standard Hours Allowed for Output, at Standard Rate

Relation between variable overhead efficiency variance and labor efficiency variance:

Problem 10-12 Name ______________________

1. a. Materials price and quantity variances:

(AQ x AP) Actual Quantity of Input, at Actual Price	(AQ x SP) Actual Quantity of Input, at Standard Price	(SQ x SP) Standard Quantity Allowed for Output, at Standard Price

b. Journal entries to record all activity relating to direct materials:

Problem 10-12 (Continued) Name ______________________

2. a. Labor rate and efficiency variances:

(AH x AR) Actual Hours of Input, at Actual Rate	(AH x SR) Actual Hours of Input, at Standard Rate	(SH x SR) Standard Hours Allowed for Output, at Standard Rate

b. Journal entry to record incurrence of direct labor cost:

Problem 10-12 (Continued) Name ______________________

3. Variable manufacturing overhead spending and efficiency variances:

(AH x AR) Actual Hours of Input, at Actual Rate	(AH x SR) Actual Hours of Input, at Standard Rate	(SH x SR) Standard Hours Allowed for Output, at Standard Rate

4. Comments on statement by company's president:

5. Possible causes of each variance:

Problem 10-13 Name ____________________

1. a. Materials price and quantity variances:

(AQ x AP) Actual Quantity of Input, at Actual Price	(AQ x SP) Actual Quantity of Input, at Standard Price	(SQ x SP) Standard Quantity Allowed for Output, at Standard Price

b. Labor rate and efficiency variances:

(AH x AR) Actual Hours of Input, at Actual Rate	(AH x SR) Actual Hours of Input, at Standard Rate	(SH x SR) Standard Hours Allowed for Output, at Standard Rate

Problem 10-13 (Continued) Name ______________________

c. Variable manufacturing overhead spending and efficiency variances:

(AH x AR) Actual Hours of Input, at Actual Rate	(AH x SR) Actual Hours of Input, at Standard Rate	(SH x SR) Standard Hours Allowed for Output, at Standard Rate

2. Summary of variances:

Materials price variance	
Materials quantity variance	
Labor rate variance	
Labor efficiency variance	
Variable overhead spending variance	
Variable overhead efficiency variance	
Net variance	

Impact on income statement:

Problem 10-13 (Continued) Name ______________________

3. Possible causes of the two most significant variances:

Problem 10-14 **Name** ______________________

1. a. b. and c.	Month			
	1	2	3	4
Throughput time in days:				
Manufacturing cycle efficiency (MCE):				
Delivery cycle time in days:				

2. Comments on trends and areas requiring improvement and recommendations:

Problem 10-14 (Continued) Name ______________________

3. a. and b.	Month	
	5	6
Throughput time in days:		
Manufacturing cycle efficiency (MCE):		

Problem 10-15 Name ______________________________

1. Standard quantity for each raw material to produce 100-liter batch:

2. Standard labor time to produce 100-liter batch:

3. Standard cost card:

	Standard Quantity or Time	Standard Price or Rate	Standard Cost

Problem 10-16 Name ______________________

1. Material price variance:

2. a. and b. Material quantity variance:

	Lot Number			Total
	30	31	32	

3. Labor efficiency variance:

4. a. and b. Labor efficiency variance:

	Lot Number			Total
	30	31	32	

Problem 10-16 (Continued) Name ____________________

5. Comments regarding expression of variances:

Problem 10-18 Name ______________________

1. Total standard cost for materials used during August:

2. Yards of material required at standard per kit:

3. Materials price and quantity variance:

(AQ x AP) Actual Quantity of Input, at Actual Price	(AQ x SP) Actual Quantity of Input, at Standard Price	(SQ x SP) Standard Quantity Allowed for Output, at Standard Price

Problem 10-18 (Continued) **Name** ______________________

4. Standard direct labor rate per hour:

5. Actual direct labor cost for the month (needed below):

Labor rate and efficiency variances:

(AH x AR) Actual Hours of Input, at Actual Rate	(AH x SR) Actual Hours of Input, at Standard Rate	(SH x SR) Standard Hours Allowed for Output, at Standard Rate

Problem 10-18 (Continued) Name ______________________________

6. Variable overhead spending and efficiency variance:

(AH x AR) Actual Hours of Input, at Actual Rate	(AH x SR) Actual Hours of Input, at Standard Rate	(SH x SR) Standard Hours Allowed for Output, at Standard Rate

7. Standard cost card for one kit:

	Standard Quantity or Hours per kit	Standard Price or Rate	Standard Cost per kit

Problem 10-19 Name ____________________

1. a. Materials price and quantity variances:

(AQ x AP) Actual Quantity of Input, at Actual Price	(AQ x SP) Actual Quantity of Input, at Standard Price	(SQ x SP) Standard Quantity Allowed for Output, at Standard Price

b. Journal entries to record direct materials activity:

Problem 10-19 (Continued) Name ____________________

2. a. Labor rate and efficiency variances:

(AH x AR) Actual Hours of Input, at Actual Rate	(AH x SR) Actual Hours of Input, at Standard Rate	(SH x SR) Standard Hours Allowed for Output, at Standard Rate

b. Journal entry to record direct labor:

3. a. Variable overhead spending and efficiency variances:

(AH x AR) Actual Hours of Input, at Actual Rate	(AH x SR) Actual Hours of Input, at Standard Rate	(SH x SR) Standard Hours Allowed for Output, at Standard Rate

b. Comments concerning labor efficiency variance and variable overhead efficiency variance:

 Name ______________________

4. For materials:

For labor:

For variable overhead:

Problem 10-20 Name ____________________

1. Materials price and quantity variances:

(AQ x AP) Actual Quantity of Input, at Actual Price	(AQ x SP) Actual Quantity of Input, at Standard Price	(SQ x SP) Standard Quantity Allowed for Output, at Standard Price

Comments concerning use of traditional variance analysis for materials:

2. Labor rate and efficiency variances:

(AH x AR) Actual Hours of Input, at Actual Rate	(AH x SR) Actual Hours of Input, at Standard Rate	(SH x SR) Standard Hours Allowed for Output, at Standard Rate

Problem 10-20 (Continued) Name ____________________

Comments concerning appropriateness of labor efficiency variance as a measure of performance:

3. Variable overhead spending and efficiency variances:

(AH x AR) Actual Hours of Input, at Actual Rate	(AH x SR) Actual Hours of Input, at Standard Rate	(SH x SR) Standard Hours Allowed for Output, at Standard Rate

Problem 10-20 (Continued) Name ______________________

Correlation between direct labor and incurrence of variable manufacturing overhead cost:

4. a. and b.

	April	May	June
Throughput time-hours:			
Manufacturing cycle efficiency (MCE):			

Problem 10-20 (Continued) **Name** ______________________

5. Conclusion concerning appropriate performance measure:

Problem 10-21 **Name** ______________________

1.

2.

3.

4.

Problem 10-22

Name ______________________________

1. a., b., and c.	Month			
	1	2	3	4
Throughput time in days:				
Manufacturing cycle efficiency (MCE):				
Delivery cycle time in days:				

2. a. Areas where the company seems to be improving:

b. Areas where the company seems to be deteriorating or stagnating:

Problem 10-22 (Continued) **Name** ______________________

2. c. Comments concerning performance:

3. a. and b.	**Month**	
	5	**6**
Throughput time in days:		
Manufacturing cycle efficiency (MCE):		

Problem 10-23 **Name** ____________________

1. Balanced scorecard:

Problem 10-23 (Continued) **Name** ______________________

2. Hypothesis underlying balanced scorecard:

3. Comments concerning management's assumptions:

Problem 10-24 Name ______________________

1. Standard cost for direct labor and materials cost components of a single jar:

Problem 10-24 (Continued) Name ____________________

2. a. Responsibility for materials price variances:

b. Responsibility for materials quantity variances:

Problem 10-25 Name ______________________________

1. Materials price and quantity variances:

(AQ x AP) Actual Quantity of Input, at Actual Price	(AQ x SP) Actual Quantity of Input, at Standard Price	(SQ x SP) Standard Quantity Allowed for Output, at Standard Price

2. Labor rate and efficiency variances:

(AH x AR) Actual Hours of Input, at Actual Rate	(AH x SR) Actual Hours of Input, at Standard Rate	(SH x SR) Standard Hours Allowed for Output, at Standard Rate

Problem 10-25 (Continued) Name ______________________

3. Variable overhead spending and efficiency variances:

(AH x AR) Actual Hours of Input, at Actual Rate	(AH x SR) Actual Hours of Input, at Standard Rate	(SH x SR) Standard Hours Allowed for Output, at Standard Rate

Case 10-26 Name ______________________________

Purchasing Department:

Manufacturing Department:

Maintenance Department:

Case 10-27 **Name** ____________________

1.

2.

Case 10-27 (Continued) Name

3.

Case 10-28 Name ______________________

1. Number of batches produced:

2. a. Gallons of Material A used in production:

b. Quantity variance for Material A:

c. Actual cost of Material A purchased:

d. Journal entries to record all activity for Material A:

Case 10-28 (Continued) Name ______________________

3. a. Standard cost per pound of Material B:

b. Pounds of Material B used in production:

Pounds of Material B allowed for production:

c. Price variance for Material B per batch:

d. Price variance for Material B:

Case 10-28 (Continued) Name ______________________

e. Journal Entries to record all activity for Material B:

4. a. Labor efficiency variance:

b. Standard hours per batch:

c. Labor rate variance:

d. Journal entries to record direct labor:

 Name ______________________

5. Standard cost of one batch:

	Standard Quantity per Batch	Price or Rate	Standard Cost per Batch

Case 10-29 Name ______________________

1.

 Name

2.

 Name ______________________________

3. a.

b.

Case 10-30 Name

Case 10-31 Name ______________________________

Problem 11-12 Name ____________________

1. Evaluation of usefulness of performance reports:

2. Recommendations:

3.

SHIPLEY COMPANY
Overhead Performance Report – Milling Department
For the Quarter Ended June 30

Problem 11-13 Name ____________________

1. Standard cost card:

2. Materials variances:

Labor variances:

3. Variable overhead variances:

(AH x AR) Actual Hours of Input, at Actual Rate	(AH x SR) Actual Hours of Input, at Standard Rate	(SH x SR) Standard Hours Allowed for Output, at Standard Rate

Problem 11-13 (Continued) Name ______________________

Fixed overhead variances:

Actual Fixed Overhead Cost	Flexible Budget Fixed Overhead Cost	Fixed Overhead Cost Applied to Work in Process

4. Effect of choice of a denominator activity level on standard unit costs:

Decision as to whether the volume variance is a controllable variance from a spending point of view:

Problem 11-14 **Name** ______________________

1.

KGV BLOODBANK
Flexible Budget Performance Report
For the Month Ended September 30

2. Variances that should be investigated:

Problem 11-15 Name ______________________

1. Direct materials variance:

2. Direct labor variances:

3. a. Variable overhead variances:

(AH x AR) Actual Hours of Input, at Actual Rate	(AH x SR) Actual Hours of Input, at Standard Rate	(SH x SR) Standard Hours Allowed for Output, at Standard Rate

Problem 11-15 (Continued) Name ______________________

b. Fixed overhead variances:

Actual Fixed Overhead Cost	Flexible Budget Fixed Overhead Cost	Fixed Overhead Cost Applied to Work in Process

Problem 11-15 (Continued) Name ______________________

4. Summary of variances:

Comments on variances:

Problem 11-16 Name ______________________

1. Predetermined overhead rate and variable and fixed cost elements:

2. Computation of "applied costs" in Manufacturing Overhead account:

3. Variable overhead variances:

(AH x AR) Actual Hours of Input, at Actual Rate	(AH x SR) Actual Hours of Input, at Standard Rate	(SH x SR) Standard Hours Allowed for Output, at Standard Rate

Problem 11-16 (Continued) Name ______________________

Fixed overhead variances:

Actual Fixed Overhead Cost	Budgeted Fixed Overhead Cost	Fixed Overhead Cost Applied to Work in Process

4. Variable overhead variances:

Spending variance:

Efficiency variance:

 Name

Fixed overhead variances:

Budget variance:

Volume variance:

Problem 11-17 Name ____________________

1. ELGIN COMPANY
Flexible Budget

2. Cost formula for all overhead costs:

Problem 11-17 Name ______________________

3.

ELGIN COMPANY
Performance Report
For the Month of May

4. Possible causes of the spending variance for supplies:

5. Efficiency variance for total variable overhead cost:

Nature of variance:

Problem 11-18 Name ______________________________

1. Evaluation of performance report:

2. See next page for performance report.

 Name ______________________

2.

MASON COMPANY

Overhead Performance Report—Milling Department

Problem 11-19 Name ______________________

1.

THE DURANT COMPANY
Flexible Budget – Machining Department

2.

THE DURANT COMPANY
Overhead Performance Report – Machining Department
For the Month Ended March 31

Problem 11-19 (Continued) **Name** ______________________

3. Additional information needed to compute overhead efficiency variance:

Problem 11-20 Name ______________________

THE ROWE COMPANY
Flexible Budget – Finishing Department

2. Predetermined overhead rate and variable and fixed cost elements:

3. a. T-account:

Manufacturing Overhead			
Actual costs	385,700		

 Name ____________________

3. b. Variable overhead variances:

(AH x AR) Actual Hours of Input, at Actual Rate	(AH x SR) Actual Hours of Input, at Standard Rate	(SH x SR) Standard Hours Allowed for Output, at Standard Rate

Fixed overhead variances:

Actual Fixed Overhead Cost	Flexible Budget Fixed Overhead Cost	Fixed Overhead Cost Applied to Work in Process

Problem 11-21 **Name** ____________________

RONSON PRODUCTS, LTD.
Overhead Performance Report – Machine Shop
For the Month Ended July 31

Problem 11-22 Name ______________________

1. Predetermined overhead rate and variable and fixed cost elements (40,000 direct labor-hours as denominator level of activity):

2. Predetermined overhead rate and variable and fixed cost elements (50,000 direct labor-hours as denominator level of activity):

3. Standard cost cards:

Denominator Activity			
40,000 DLHs		50,000 DLHs	
Direct materials		Direct materials	
Direct labor		Direct labor	
Variable overhead		Variable overhead	
Fixed overhead		Fixed overhead	
Total standard cost per unit		Total standard cost per unit	

4. a. Standard hours allowed for the year's production:

4. b. T-account:

Manufacturing Overhead		
Actual costs	446,500	

Problem 11-22 (Continued) Name ____________________

4. c. Variable overhead variances:

(AH x AR) Actual Hours of Input, at Actual Rate	(AH x SR) Actual Hours of Input, at Standard Rate	(SH x SR) Standard Hours Allowed for Output, at Standard Rate

Fixed overhead variances:

Actual Fixed Overhead Cost	Flexible Budget Fixed Overhead Cost	Fixed Overhead Cost Applied to Work in Process

5. Major disadvantage and offsetting advantages:

Problem 11-23 Name ______________________

1. Predetermined overhead rate and variable and fixed cost elements:

2. Standard cost card:

3. a. Standard direct labor-hours allowed for the year's production:

b. T-account:

Manufacturing Overhead

4. Variable overhead variances:

(AH x AR) Actual Hours of Input, at Actual Rate	(AH x SR) Actual Hours of Input, at Standard Rate	(SH x SR) Standard Hours Allowed for Output, at Standard Rate

Problem 11-23 (Continued) **Name** ______________________

Fixed overhead variances:

Actual Fixed Overhead Cost	Flexible Budget Fixed Overhead Cost	Fixed Overhead Cost Applied to Work in Process

5. Effect of change in denominator activities on variance(s):

Problem 11-24 Name ______________________

1. Predetermined overhead rate and variable and fixed cost elements:

2. Standard cost card:

3. See next page for graph.

4. a. Fixed overhead variances:

Actual Fixed Overhead Cost	Flexible Budget Fixed Overhead Cost	Fixed Overhead Cost Applied to Work in Process

Problem 11-24 (Continued) Name ______________________

3.

Problem 11-24 (Continued) Name ______________________

4. b. Variable overhead variances:

(AH x AR) Actual Hours of Input, at Actual Rate	(AH x SR) Actual Hours of Input, at Standard Rate	(SH x SR) Standard Hours Allowed for Output, at Standard Rate

Problem 11-24 (Continued) Name ______________________________

5. a. Fixed overhead variances:

Actual Fixed Overhead Cost	Flexible Budget Fixed Overhead Cost	Fixed Overhead Cost Applied to Work in Process

b. Variable overhead variances:

(AH x AR) Actual Hours of Input, at Actual Rate	(AH x SR) Actual Hours of Input, at Standard Rate	(SH x SR) Standard Hours Allowed for Output, at Standard Rate

Problem 11-25

Name ______________________

1. Computations of cost formulas:

	Cost	Variable with respect to	Activity level	Cost per unit of activity
Actors and directors' wages				
Stagehands' wages				
Ticket booth personnel and ushers' wages				
Scenery, costumes, and props				
Theater hall rent				
Printed programs				
Publicity				
Administrative expenses (15%)				
Administrative expenses (10%)				
Fixed administrative expenses (75%)				

2. See next page for performance report.

3. Comments on cost control:

4. Accuracy of cost formula figures for predicting costs:

Problem 11-25 (Continued) **Name** ______________________

2.

THE MUNCHKIN THEATER
Performance Report
For 2003

Case 11-26 **Name** ______________________

Case 11-27 Name ______________________

1. Number of units produced:

2. and 3. Direct materials variances (computation of yards purchased and used in production and actual cost per yard):

Actual Quantity of Inputs, at Actual Price (AQ x AP)	Actual Quantity of Inputs, at Standard Price (AQ x SP)	Standard Quantity Allowed for Output, at Standard Price (SQ x SP)

Case 11-27 (Continued) Name ______________________

4. and 5. Direct labor variances (computation of actual direct labor hours worked and actual rate per direct labor-hours):

Actual Hours of Input, at Actual Rate (AH x AR)	Actual Hours of Input, at Standard Rate (AH x SR)	Standard Hours Allowed for Output, at Standard Rate (SH x SR)

6. Variable overhead variances (computation of actual variable overhead cost incurred):

(AH x AR) Actual Hours of Input, at Actual Rate	(AH x SR) Actual Hours of Input, at Standard Rate	(SH x SR) Standard Hours Allowed for Output, at Standard Rate

 Name ____________________

7. Fixed overhead variances (computation of total fixed manufacturing overhead cost in flexible budget):

Actual Fixed Overhead Cost	Flexible Budget Fixed Overhead Cost	Fixed Overhead Cost Applied to Work in Process

8. Denominator hours:

Case 11-28 Name ____________________

1. Benefits of flexible budgeting:

2.

SOFTGROW, INC.
Revised Monthly Selling Expense Report
November

See supporting calculations on next page.

Case 11-28 (Continued) **Name** ______________________

Calculations:

Case 11-29 Name ______________________________

	Company X	Company Y
1. Denominator activity in machine-hours		
2. Standard machine-hours allowed for units produced		
3. Actual machine-hours worked		
4. Flexible budget variable overhead per machine-hour		
5. Flexible budget fixed overhead (total)		
6. Actual variable overhead cost		
7. Actual fixed overhead cost		
8. Variable overhead cost applied to production		
9. Fixed overhead cost applied to production		
10. Variable overhead spending variance		
11. Variable overhead efficiency variance		
12. Fixed overhead budget variance		
13. Fixed overhead volume variance		
14. Variable portion of the predetermined overhead rate		
15. Fixed portion of the predetermined overhead rate		
16. Underapplied (or overapplied) overhead		

Calculations:

Case 11-29 (Continued) Name ______________________

Calculations:

Group Exercise 11-30 Name ______________________________

1. a. Negative behavioral implications:

b. Method(s) to reduce negative behavioral effects:

2. How tight cost standards can have positive behavioral effects:

3. Participants in setting standards:

Benefits of their participation in standard setting process:

Group Exercise 11-31

Name ______________________________

Group Exercise 11-31 (Continued) **Name** ______

Problem 12-14 Name ____________________

1. Segmented Income Statements

	Total Company		Sales Territory			
			Central		Eastern	
	Amount	%	Amount	%	Amount	%

	Central Territory		Product Line			
			Awls		Pows	
	Amount	%	Amount	%	Amount	%

Problem 12-14 (Continued)   Name ____________________

2. Observations concerning total company segmented by territory:

3. Observations concerning Central Territory segmented by product line:

Problem 12-15 Name ____________________

1. Segmented Income Statement:

Flour		Pancake Mix		Wheat Cereal		Total Company	
%	Amount	%	Amount	%	Amount	%	Amount

Name

2. a. Comments concerning decision to eliminate wheat cereal:

2. b. Comments concerning decision to focus all efforts on promoting pancake mix:

3. Recommendations:

Problem 12-16 **Name** ______________________________

1. Disadvantages or weakness of existing statement format:

2. Basis used to allocate corporate expenses to territories:

Problem 12-16 (Continued) **Name** ____________________

3. Revised segmented income statement:

	Total		Southern Europe		Middle Europe		Northern Europe	
	Amount	%	Amount	%	Amount	%	Amount	%

Problem 12-16 (Continued) Name ______________________

4. Analysis of new segmented income statement:

Problem 12-17 Name ______________________________

1. Advantages in breaking ROI computation into two separate elements:

2.

	Company		
	A	B	C
Sales	4,000,000	1,500,000	
Net operating income	560,000	210,000	
Average operating assets	2,000,000		3,000,000
Margin			3.5%
Turnover			2%
ROI		7%	

Problem 12-17 (Continued) **Name** ______________________

Comments on relative performance and recommendations:

Problem 12-18 Name ____________________

1.

	Present	New Line	Total

Calculation of net operating income for new line (for use above):

2. Fred Halloway's decision to accept or reject new product line:

3. Headquarter's justification for accepting East Division's new product line:

4. a. East Division's residual income:

	Present	New Line	Total

Problem 12-18 (Continued) **Name** ____________________

b. Fred Halloway's decision to accept or reject new product line:

Problem 12-19 Name ______________________

1. Total operating assets

	Ending Balances	Beginning Balances

Average operating assets:

Margin:

Turnover:

ROI:

2. Residual income:

Problem 12-20 Name

1. Transfer price range and comments:

2. a. Division A's determination of transfer price:

Division B's determination of transfer price:

Comments:

b. Loss in potential profits for company as a whole if transfer price of $380 per unit is rejected by Division B:

Problem 12-20 (Continued) Name

3. a. Transfer price range and comments:

b. Impact on ROI if Division A accepts transfer price of $52 per unit:

4. Lowest acceptable transfer price from Division A's perspective:

Problem 12-21 Name ____________________

1. Tuner Division's determination of transfer price:

Assembly Division's determination of transfer price:

Comments:

2. Effect on profits of Tuner Division and company as a whole if Tuner Division meets price being paid to overseas supplier:

Problem 12-21 (Continued) Name

3. Transfer price range and comments:

4. Decision by Tuner Division to meet price of overseas supplier and effect on profits of the company as a whole if price is met:

5. Impact of decision to force Assembly Division to purchase from the Tuner Division at a higher price for the company as a whole:

6. Effect of decision to require Assembly Division to purchase 30,000 tuners at $20 per tuner from the Tuner Division on the company as a whole:

Problem 12-22 Name ______________________

1. Segmented income statement for Leather Division:

	Leather Division		Product Line					
			Garments		Shoes		Handbags	
	Amount	%	Amount	%	Amount	%	Amount	%

Problem 12-22 (Continued) **Name** ______________________

2. Segmented income statement for handbag product lines:

	Handbags		Sales Market			
			Domestic		Foreign	
	Amount	%	Amount	%	Amount	%

3. Decision concerning special promotional campaign and supporting computations:

Problem 12-23 **Name** ______________________________

1. Segmented income statement (contribution format):

	Total Company		District A		District B		District C	
	Amount	%	Amount	%	Amount	%	Amount	%

Problem 12-23 (Continued) Name ______________________

2. Contribution margin per order for each district:

	District A	District B	District C

Problems suggested by computation:

3. Justification for expenditure for special promotional campaign:

 Name ______________________

4. Analysis of segmented income statement (prepared in part 1):

Problem 12-24 Name ______________________

1. Presser Division's average operating assets:

Presser Division's ROI:

b. Presser Division's residual income:

2. Decision concerning investment opportunity with ROI of 18% if residual income is used as performance measure rather than ROI:

3. Items Presser Division must be free to control if performance is evaluated by either the ROI or residual income performance measures:

Problem 12-25 Name ______________________

1. ROI:

2. Impact of cost savings of $10,000 on ROI:

3. Impact of reduction in average inventory of $100,000 on ROI:

4. Impact of increase in sales of $100,000 on ROI:

5. Impact of purchase of machinery using proceeds of $125,000 from issuance of bonds and resulting $5,000 reduction in production costs on ROI:

6. Impact of purchase of land for possible use in future using $180,000 collected from customers on account on ROI:

Problem 12-25 (Continued) **Name** ______________________

7. Impact of write-off of $20,000 of obsolete inventory on ROI:

Problem 12-26 Name ____________________

1. Required sales (in units) to obtain desired rate of return on assets:

a. Margin earned at this sales level:

b. Turnover at this sales level:

2. a. and b. Margin, turnover and ROI

	Sales Volume		
Units sold	160000	180000	200000

3. Margin, turnover and ROI:

	Present Sales	New Sales	Total Sales
Units sold	180000	20000	200000

Problem 12-26 (Continued) **Name** ______________________

Recommendation:

Problem 12-27 **Name** ______________________

1. Decision to accept or reject $400 price:

2. Impact of rejecting $400 price (and supporting computations):

Problem 12-27 (Continued) Name ____________________

3. Impact of accepting $400 price (and supporting computations):

4. Conclusions:

Problem 12-28 Name

1. Lowest acceptable transfer price:

2. Effect on profits of company as a whole if Compressor Division meets price:

Problem 12-29 **Name** ______________________________

1. Segmented income statement:

	Total	Membership Services	Journal	Books and Reports	Continuing Education

See supporting computations on next page.

Problem 12-29 (Continued) **Name** ______________________

Supporting computations:

2. Arguments for and against allocation of all costs of the Association to the four programs:

Case 12-30 **Name** ______________________

1. Recommendation:

2. Recommendation:

Case 12-30 (Continued) Name ______________________

3. Transfer price range and discussion:

4. Discussion of organizational and manages behavioral problems and advice:

Case 12-31 **Name** ____________________

1. Segmented income statement:

	Total		Line A		Line B		Line C	
	Amount	%	Amount	%	Amount	%	Amount	%

Case 12-31 (Continued) Name ______________________________

2. Comments concerning decision to cut back production of line A:

3. Advantages and disadvantages of eliminating line C:

Case 12-31 (Continued) Name ____________________

4. a. Segmented income statement:

	Total		Home Market		Foreign Market	
	Amount	%	Amount	%	Amount	%

Case 12-31 (Continued) Name ______________________________

4. b. Analysis of segmented income statement:

Group Exercise 12-32 Name

1.

 Name ________________

2.

Problem 13-11 Name ______________________

1. Impact on company profits if tour is discontinued:

The following costs are not relevant to the decision:

Cost	Reason

2. Potential effects of elimination of lower-than-average seat occupancy tours:

Problem 13-12 Name ______________________________

1. Effect on net operating income of company as a whole if Bath Department is dropped:

2. Decision to process further or sell merifulon at split-off point (and supporting computation):

3. Order of acceptance of orders for X, Y, and Z (and support computations):

	X	Y	Z

 Name ______________________

4. Dollar advantage or disadvantage of accepting supplier's order:

	Relevant Costs	
	Make	Buy

5. Effect on monthly profits if order is accepted:

	Per Unit	Total for 2,000 Units

6. Relevant cost for establishing minimum selling price:

Problem 13-13 **Name** ______________________

1. Profit per pound from processing further:

2. Recommendation:

Problem 13-14 **Name** ______________________

1. Recommendation and supporting computations:

2. Levels of sales (in gallons) for the two-month period at which company will be indifferent between closing plant and keeping it open:

Supporting computations:

	Operate at 12,000 Gallons for Two Months	Close for Two Months

Problem 13-15 Name ______________________

1. Decision to accept or reject outside supplier's offer (and supporting computations):

Problem 13-15 (Continued) **Name** ______________________

2. Maximum price company will be willing to pay outside supplier:

3. Costs under alternative #1 – produce all cartridges internally:

Costs under alternative #2 – purchase all cartridges externally:

Costs under alternative #3 – produce 100,000 boxes internally and purchase 50,000 boxes externally:

4. Qualitative factors to be considered:

Problem 13-16 **Name** ______________________

1. Effect on net operating income if only 40,000 units are produced and sold:

2. Effect on net operating income if the 10,000 units were sold through regular channels:

Problem 13-17 Name ____________________

1. Impact on overall company net income if Downtown Store were closed:

2. Recommendation:

3. Impact on overall company net income if Downtown Store were closed and sales in Uptown Store increased by $200,000 per quarter:

Problem 13-18 Name ____________________

1. Recommendation:

Supporting computations:

	Differential Costs Per Unit		Total Differential Costs— 40,000 Units	
	Make	Buy	Make	Buy

Problem 13-18 (Continued) Name ______________________________

2. a. Recommendation (assuming 50,000 subassemblies per year):

Supporting computations:

	Differential Costs Per Unit		Total Differential Costs—50,000 Units	
	Make	Buy	Make	Buy

Problem 13-18 (Continued) Name ______________________

b. Recommendation (assuming 60,000 subassemblies per year):

	Differential Costs Per Unit		Total Differential Costs—60,000 Units	
	Make	Buy	Make	Buy

3. Other factors to be considered:

Problem 13-19 Name ____________________

1. Recommendation concerning $150,000 increase in fixed selling expenses:

Supporting computations:

2. Break-even price per unit on overseas order:

3. Dollar advantage or disadvantage of closing plant for the three-month period:

Problem 13-19 **Name** ______________________

4. Unit cost figure that is relevant for setting minimum selling price:

5. Unit cost figure that is relevant for comparison to an outside quoted price:

Problem 13-20 **Name** ______________________________

1. Avoidable costs:

The following costs are not relevant to the decision:

Cost	Reason

Recommendation and supporting computation:

2. Classification of avoidable costs:

	Variable	Fixed

Recommendation:

Contribution margin ratio:

Break-even point:

Problem 13-21 **Name** ______________________

1. Contribution margin per direct labor-hour expended on each product:

Sewing Kit	
Lenny	
Cari	
Tina	
Marcy	

Problem 13-21 (Continued) Name ____________________

2. Schedule of direct labor-hours required to produce units estimated to be sold:

Product	DLH Per Unit	Estimated Sales	Total
Marcy			
Tina			
Cari			
Lenny			
Sewing Kit			
Total DLHs required			

3. Amount of each product to be made so that its total production time is equal to the 150,000 direct labor-hours available:

4. Highest price, in terms of rate per hour, to be paid for additional capacity:

5. Ways that the company could obtain additional output:

Problem 13-22 Name ______________________

1. Incremental contribution margin per container from further processing of the honey into candies:

Problem 13-22 (Continued) Name ______________________

2. Minimum number of containers of candy that must be sold to justify the continued processing of honey into candies:

Case 13-23 Name ______________________

1. Recommendation (including discussion of relevant costs and supporting computations:

Case 13-23 (Continued) Name ______________________

2. Comments about vice president's decision to shut down the Ashton facility:

3. Influence of depreciation of Ashton facility on prices charged:

Problem 13-24 Name ______________________

Definition of the two alternatives with relevant data (starting point):

Alternative A:

Alternative B:

Identification of cost(s) and other factor(s) that are not relevant (starting point):

See part 1 on next page.

 Name

1. Recommendation as to which order should be accepted:

Supporting computations:

2. Comments concerning impact of acceptance of order from the Wales Company on Whitmore Products as a whole:

See supporting computations on next page.

 Name ______________________

Supporting computations:

Alternative A:

Alternative B:

Case 13-25 Name ______________________

1. Lowest price that company could bid without reducing net income:

Case 13-25 (Continued) Name ______________________

2. Price to be quoted for new compound:

Case 13-26 **Name** ______________________

1. Recommendation (and supporting computations):

2. Lowest price that should be accepted for a ton of flour:

Case 13-27 Name

1. Advantages of obtaining covers from Greenville Cover Plant:

2. a. Total annual relevant costs:

b. Total annual continuing costs:

Case 13-27 (Continued) Name ____________________

2. c. Nonrecurring costs that would arise due to closing of plant:

Relevance of nonrecurring costs to the decision:

3. Recommendation:

Supporting computations:

	First Year	Other Years

4. Other factors to be considered:

Case 13-28 Name ______________________

1. Usefulness of data submitted by accounting department:

2. Contribution margin per unit (assuming direct labor is a fixed cost):

	Purchased XSX Drums	Manufactured XSX Drums	Manufactured Mountain Bike Frames

3. Contribution margin per welding hour (assuming direct labor is a fixed cost):

	Manufactured XSX Drums	Manufactured Mountain Bike Frames

Case 13-28 **Name** ______________________

3. (Continued) Effect on contribution margin and net operating income (assuming direct labor is a fixed cost):

	Quantity	Unit Contribution Margin	Welding Time per Unit	Total Welding Time	Balance of Welding	Total Contribution

4. Contribution margin per unit (assuming direct labor is a variable cost):

		Manufactured	
	Purchased XSX Drums	XSX Drums	Mountain Bike Frames

Contribution margin per welding hour (assuming direct labor is a variable cost):

	Manufactured	
	XSX Drums	Mountain Bike Frames

Case 13-28 (Continued) Name ____________________

Effect on contribution margin and net operating income (assuming direct labor is a variable cost):

	Quantity	Unit Contri-bution Margin	Welding Time per Unit	Total Welding Time	Balance of Welding	Total Contri-bution

5. Treatment of direct labor as a variable cost or as a fixed cost:

Group Exercise 13-29 Name ______________________________

1. Meaning of manufacturing overhead rates of 500% or more of direct labor:

2. Implications of such high manufacturing overhead rates:

3. Impact of outsourcing on costs of remaining products:

4. Drawbacks and limitations:

5. Consequences:

Problem 14-16 Name ______________________

1. Annual cash inflows:

2. Net present value:

Item	Year(s)	Amount of Cash Flows	Factor	Present Value of Cash Flows

Problem 14-17 Name ______________________

1. Net annual cost savings:

2. Net present value:

Item	Year(s)	Amount of Cash Flows	Factor	Present Value of Cash Flows

Recommendation:

3. Dollar value of intangible benefits:

Problem 14-18 Name

1. Income statement:

2. Simple rate of return:

Recommendation:

Problem 14-18 (Continued) **Name** ______________________

3. Payback period:

Recommendation:

Problem 14-19 **Name** ____________________

Net present value:

Item	Year(s)	Amount of Cash Flows	Factor	Present Value of Cash Flows

Recommendation:

Problem 14-20 Name ______________________

1. Formula for profitability index:

Profitability index for each project:

Project 1:

Project 2:

Project 3:

Project 4:

Project 5:

2. a., b., and c. Rankings:

	Net Present Value	Profitability Index	Internal Rate of Return
First preference			
Second preference			
Third preference			
Fourth preference			
Fifth preference			

3. Comments about approaches used to rank projects:

Problem 14-21 **Name** ______________________________

Net present value:

Items and Computations	Year(s)	Amount	Tax Effect	After-Tax Cash Flows	Factor	Present Value of Cash Flows

Recommendation:

Problem 14-22 Name ______________________

1. Expected net annual cash receipts:

2. Net present value:

Item	Year(s)	Amount of Cash Flows	Factor	Present Value of Cash Flows

Recommendation:

Problem 14-23 Name ____________________

1. Internal rate of return:

Verification (net present value):

Item	Year(s)	Amount of Cash Flows	Factor	Present Value of Cash Flows

2. Annual cash inflow that would provide return of 14%:

Problem 14-23 (Continued) Name ______________

3. a. Internal rate of return (5-year life):

Internal rate of return (9-year life):

Comments:

4. a. Internal rate of return (assuming annual cash inflow is 20% greater than expected):

b. Internal rate of return (assuming annual cash inflow is 20% less than expected):

Problem 14-23 (Continued) Name ______________________

5. Internal rate of return:

Verification (net present value):

Item	Year(s)	Amount of Cash Flows	Factor	Present Value of Cash Flows

Problem 14-24 **Name** ______________________

1. **Formula for profitability index:**

Profitability index for each project:

Project A:

Project B:

Project C:

Project D:

Project E:

2. **a., b., and c. Rankings:**

	Net Present Value	Profitability Index	Internal Rate of Return
First preference			
Second preference			
Third preference			
Fourth preference			
Fifth preference			

Problem 14-24 (Continued) Name ______________________

3. Comments about approaches used to rank projects:

Problem 14-25 **Name** ____________________

1. Income statement:

2. Simple rate of return:

Recommendation:

3. Payback period:

Recommendation:

Problem 14-26 Name ______________________

1. Net present value (total-cost approach):

Item	Year(s)	Amount of Cash Flows	Factor	Present Value of Cash Flows
Purchase new generator:				
Keep old generator:				

Recommendation: ______________________

Problem 14-26 (Continued) Name ______________________

2. Net present value (incremental-cost approach):

Item	Year(s)	Amount of Cash Flows	Factor	Present Value of Cash Flows

Problem 14-27 Name ______________________________

1. Annual net savings in cash operating costs if machine is purchased:

2. Simple rate of return:

3. Payback period:

Recommendation:

Problem 14-27 (Continued) Name ____________________

4. Internal rate of return:

Comments regarding use of simple rate of return as guide in investment decisions:

Problem 14-28 Name ______________________

1. Net present value:

Items and Computations	Year(s)	Amount	Tax Effect	After-Tax Cash Flows	Factor	Present Value of Cash Flows

2. Recommendation:

Problem 14-29 Name ______________________

Net present value (total-cost approach):

Item	Year(s)	Amount of Cash Flows	Factor	Present Value of Cash Flows
Purchase alternative:				
Lease alternative:				

Recommendation:

Problem 14-30 **Name** ____________________

1. Net annual cost savings:

2. Net present value:

Item	Year(s)	Amount of Cash Flows	Factor	Present Value of Cash Flows

3. Net annual cost savings:

3. (continued) Recomputation of net present value:

Item	Year(s)	Amount of Cash Flows	Factor	Present Value of Cash Flows

Comments about whether company made a wise investment:

4. a. Other benefits that might accrue:

b. Cash inflow required to yield 20% rate of return:

Problem 14-31 **Name** ______________________

Items and Computations	Year(s)	Amount	Tax Effect	After-Tax Cash Flows	Factor	Present Value of Cash Flows
Alternative 1:						
Alternative 2:						

Net present value:

Problem 14-31 (Continued) **Name** ______________________

Recommendation:

Problem 14-32 Name ______________________

1. Net cash inflows:

	Year			
	1	2	3	4

Problem 14-32 (Continued) **Name** ______________________

2. Net present value:

Item	Year(s)	Amount of Cash Flows	Factor	Present Value of Cash Flows

Recommendation:

Case 14-33 Name ______________________

1. Recommendation:

Case 14-33 (Continued) Name ______________________

2. Suggestions for revising the way in which postaudits are conducted:

Case 14-34 **Name** ______________________________

1.

Item	Year(s)	Amount of Cash Flows	Factor	Present Value of Cash Flows

2. Reply regarding building's future sales value:

Case 14-35 Name ______________________

1. Annual production costs:

	Year(s)			
	1	2	3	4-10
Units produced				
Model 2600: Total cost at $0.90 per unit				
Model 5600: Total cost at $0.70 per unit				

Net present value (using either total-cost or incremental-cost approach):

Item	Year(s)	Amount of Cash Flows	Factor	Present Value of Cash Flows

Case 14-35 (Continued) Name ______________________

2. Impact of increase in cost of materials on desirability of Model 5200:

3. Impact of increase in cost of labor on desirability of Model 5200:

Case 14-36 Name ____________________

1. Net present value:

Items and computations	Year(s)	Amount of Cash Flows	Factor	Present Value of Cash Flows

Case 14-36 (Continued) Name ______________________

2. Required market price to break even:

Group Exercise 14-37 Name ____________________

Group Exercise 14-37 (Continued) Name

Problem 15-8 Name ____________________

1. Step method:

Assembly

Stamping

Maintenance

Personnel

Custodial Services

Factory Admin.

Problem 15-8 (Continued) **Name** ____________________

2. Direct method:

Assembly	
Stamping	
Maintenance	
Personnel	
Custodial Services	
Factory Admin.	

Problem 15-8 (Continued) Name

3. Plantwide rate:

4. Amount of overhead assigned to job:

Step method:

Direct method

Plant-wide method:

Problem 15-9 Name ______________________

1. Planned allocation of maintenance department costs:

	Machine Tools	Special Products

2. Allocation of actual maintenance department costs:

	Machine Tools	Special Products

3. Allocation to each division (assuming allocation in proportion to actual machine-hours recorded):

4. Criticism of allocation method:

5. Probable strategy and suggestion:

Problem 15-10 **Name** ______________________________

1. Beginning of year allocation of budgeted cafeteria cost:

	Milling Department	Finishing Department	Total

2. a. End of year allocation of actual cafeteria costs:

	Milling Department	Finishing Department	Total

Problem 15-10 (Continued) **Name** ______________________

b. Portion of actual cafeteria costs not allocated:

	Variable Cost	Fixed Cost	Total

Explanation:

Problem 15-11 Name ______________________

1. Comments about Merit's complaint:

2. Monthly cost of computer (using high-low method):

Problem 15-11 (Continued) **Name** ____________________

3. Reallocation of costs:

	Division			
	Lending	Retail	Commercial	Total

Problem 15-12 **Name** ____________________

1.

	Food Services	Admin. Services	X-Ray Services	Out-Pat. Clinic	OB Care	General Hospital
Variable costs						

Problem 15-12 (Continued) Name ____________________

2.

	Food Services	Admin. Services	X-Ray Services	Out-Pat. Clinic	OB Care	General Hospital
Fixed costs						

Problem 15-13 **Name** ____________________

	Variable costs	Grounds & Maint.	General Admin.	Laundry	Convention Center	Food Services	Lodging

Problem 15-13 (Continued)

Name ______________________________

	Grounds & Maint.	General Admin.	Laundry	Convention Center	Food Services	Lodging
Fixed costs						

Problem 15-14 Name ______________________

1. and 2. Allocation of costs:

	Medical Services	Maintenance	Metals	Plastics
Variable costs to be allocated				
Fixed costs to be allocated				

Problem 15-14 (Continued) Name

Supporting computations:

3. Planned cost of one unit of product in Plastics Department:

Case 15-15 Name ______________________________

	Cafeteria	Custodial Services	Machinery Maintenance	Milling	Finishing
1. Step method:					

	Cafeteria	Custodial Services	Machinery Maintenance	Milling	Finishing
2. Direct method:					

Case 15-15 (Continued) **Name** ______________________

3. a. Amount of overhead cost assigned to the job:

b. Explanation:

Case 15-16 Name ______________________

1. Computation of plantwide rate:

2. a. Allocation rates for variable service department costs:

Case 15-16 (Continued) **Name** ______________________

2. a. (Continued) Allocation of service department costs using direct method:

Finishing
Assembly
Molding
Maintenance
Quality Control

2. b. Overhead rates:

	Molding	Assembly	Finishing

3. a. Overhead costs allocated to Pipeline Model (using plantwide overhead rate):

3. b. Effects of use of plantwide rate to allocate overhead:

Case 15-16 (Continued) **Name** ______________________

4. Additional steps required:

Group Exercise 15-17

Name ____________________

Group Exercise 15-17 (Continued) Name

Problem 16-9 Name ____________________

Transaction	Activity			Source, Use Or Neither	Separate Schedule
	Operating	Investing	Financing		
a. Bonds were retired by paying the principal amount due					
b. Equipment was purchased by giving a long-term note to the seller					
c. Interest was paid on a note, decreasing Interest Payable					
d. Accrued taxes were paid					
e. A long-term loan was made to a supplier					
f. Interest was received on the loan in (e) above, reducing Interest Receivable					
g. Cash dividends were declared and paid					
h. A building was acquired in exchange for shares of the company's common stock					
i. Common stock was sold for cash to investors					
j. Equipment was sold for cash					
k. Equipment was sold in exchange for a long-term note					
l. Convertible bonds were converted into common stock					

Problem 16-10 Name ______________________

(Note: An optional worksheet, which may be used to organize the data, appears on the next page.)

1. and 2.

EATON COMPANY
Statement of Cash Flows
For the Year Ended December 31, 2002

Name ____________________

EATON COMPANY
Optional Worksheet for Preparation of Statement of Cash Flows
For the Year Ended December 31, 2002

	Change	Source or Use	Cash Flow Effect	Adjustments	Adjusted Effect	Classi-fication

Problem 16-11 **Name** ______________________

1. Cash basis income statement (using direct method):

Problem 16-11 (Continued) Name ______________________

2.

EATON COMPANY
Statement of Cash Flows
For the Year Ended December 31, 2002

Problem 16-12 Name ____________________

(Note: An optional worksheet, which may be used to organize the data, follows part 3.)

1. and 2.

FOXBORO COMPANY
Statement of Cash Flows
For Year 2

3. Explanation as to why cash declined so sharply during the year:

Name ______________________________

FOXBORO COMPANY
Optional Worksheet for Preparation of Statement of Cash Flows
For Year 2

	Change	Source or Use	Cash Flow Effect	Adjustments	Adjusted Effect	Classi-fication

Problem 16-13 Name ______________________________

1. Cash basis income statement (using direct method):

Problem 16-13 (Continued) Name ______________________

2.

FOXBORO COMPANY
Statement of Cash Flows
For Year 2

 Name

3. Explanation as to why cash declined so sharply during the year:

Problem 16-14 Name ______________________

(Note: An optional worksheet, which may be used to organize the date, follows part 3.)
1. and 2.

ALLIED PROUCTS
Statement of Cash Flows
For the Year Ended December 31, 2002

Problem 16-14 (Continued) **Name** ______________________

3. Major reasons for decline in company's cash position:

Problem 16-14 (Continued) Name ______________________________

ALLIED PRODUCTS
Optional Worksheet for Preparation of Statement of Cash Flows
For the Year Ended December 31, 2002

	Change	Source or Use	Cash Flow Effect	Adjustments	Adjusted Effect	Classification

Problem 16-15 **Name** ____________________

1. Cash basis income statement (using direct method):

 Name ______________________

2.

ALLIED PRODUCTS
Statement of Cash Flows
For the Year Ended December 31, 2002

Problem 16-16 Name

Determination of missing amounts:

Problem 16-16 (Continued) Name ____________________

(Note: An optional worksheet, which may be used to organize the date, appears on the following page.)

DAMOCLES COMPANY
Statement of Cash Flows
For the Year

Problem 16-16 (Continued) Name ______________________

DAMOCLES COMPANY
Optional Worksheet for Preparation of Statement of Cash Flows
For the Year

	Change	Source or Use	Cash Flow Effect	Adjustments	Adjusted Effect	Classi-fication

Problem 16-17 Name ______________________________

ALCORN PRODUCTS
Worksheet for Preparation of Statement of Cash Flows
For the Year Ended December 31, 2002

	Change	Source or Use	Cash Flow Effect	Adjustments	Adjusted Effect	Classification

ALCORN PRODUCTS
Worksheet for Preparation of Statement of Cash Flows (continued)
For the Year Ended December 31, 2002

	Change	Source or Use	Cash Flow Effect	Adjustments	Adjusted Effect	Classi-fication

2.

ALCORN PRODUCTS
Statement of Cash Flows
For the Year Ended December 31, 2002

Problem 16-17 (Continued) **Name** ____________________

3. Problems revealed by statement of cash flows:

Problem 16-18 Name ______________________

Cash basis income statement (direct method):

Problem 16-19 **Name** ______________________

Determination of missing amounts:

Problem 16-19 (Continued) Name ____________________

(Note: An optional worksheet, which may be used to organize the data, appears on the next page.)

LUANG CORP.
Statement of Cash Flows
For the Past Year

Problem 16-19 (Continued) Name ____________________

LUANG CORP.
Optional Worksheet for Preparation of Statement of Cash Flows
For the Past Year

	Change	Source or Use	Cash Flow Effect	Adjustments	Adjusted Effect	Classification

Problem 16-19 (Continued) **Name** ______________________________

LUANG CORP.
Optional Worksheet for Preparation of Statement of Cash Flows (continued)
For the Past Year

	Change	Source or Use	Cash Flow Effect	Adjustments	Adjusted Effect	Classi-fication

Group Exercise 16-20

Name ______________________________

Group Exercise 16-20 (Continued) Name ______________________

Problem 17-8 Name ______________________

1. Net income to the common stockholders:

	Method A	Method B	Method C

2. Return on common equity:

3. Comments regarding methods A, B and C:

Problem 17-9 Name ______________________

1. a. Computation of working capital:

b. Computation of current ratio:

c. Computation of acid-test ratio:

Problem 17-9 (Continued)　　Name ______________________

2.

	Effect on		
	Working Capital	Current Ratio	Acid-Test Ratio
(a) Declared a cash dividend			
(b) Paid accounts payable			
(c) Collected cash on accounts receivable			
(d) Purchased equipment for cash			
(e) Paid a cash dividend previously declared			
(f) Borrowed cash on a short-term note			
(g) Sold inventory at a profit			
(h) Wrote-off uncollectible accounts			
(i) Sold marketable securities at a loss			
(j) Issued capital stock for cash			
(k) Paid off short-term notes			

Problem 17-10 Name ______________________

1.

	This Year	Last Year
a. Working capital:		
b. Current ratio:		
c. Acid-test ratio:		
d. Average age of receivables:		
e. Inventory turnover in days:		
f. Debt-to-equity ratio:		
g. Times interest earned:		

Problem 17-10 (Continued) **Name** ______________________

2. a.

MODERN BUILDING SUPPLY
Common-Size Balance Sheets

	This Year %	Last Year %

b. **MODERN BUILDING SUPPLY**
Common-Size Income Statements

	This Year					Last Year				
					%					%

Problem 17-10 (Continued) **Name** ______________________

3. Problems or strengths and recommendations:

Problem 17-11 **Name** ______________________

1.

	This Year	Last Year
a. Earnings per share:		
b. Dividend yield ratio:		
c. Dividend payment ratio:		
d. Price-earnings ratio:		

Investors' view of company as compared to others in industry:

Problem 17-11 (Continued) Name ______________________

1.

	This Year	Last Year
e. Book value per share:		

Comments regarding current price of common stock:

2.

a. Return on total assets:		
b. Return on common equity:		

Problem 17-11 (Continued) Name ______________________

c. Comments regarding financial leverage:

3. Problems or strengths and recommendations:

Problem 17-12 Name ______________________

1.

	This Year	Last Year
a. Return on total assets:		
b. Return on common equity:		

c. Comments regarding company's leverage:

Problem 17-12 (Continued) Name ____________________

2.

	This Year	Last Year
a. Earnings per share:		
b. Dividend yield ratio:		
c. Dividend payout ratio:		

d. Investors' view of company as compared to others in industry:

(Note: Parts e and f are on the next page.)

Problem 17-12 (Continued) Name ______________________

	This Year	Last Year
e. Book value per share of common:		

Comments regarding current price of common stock:

f. Gross margin percentage:

(Note: Part 3 is on the next page.)

Problem 17-12 (Continued) Name ____________________

3.

	This Year	Last Year
a. Working capital:		
b. Current ratio:		
c. Acid-test ratio:		
d. Average age of receivables:		
e. Inventory turnover:		
f. Debt-to-equity ratio:		
g. Times interest earned:		

Problem 17-12 (Continued) Name ______________________

4. Recommendation regarding approval of loan:

Problem 17-13 **Name** ______________________________

1.

HEDRICK COMPANY
Comparative Balance Sheets

	This Year	Last Year

Problem 17-13 (Continued) **Name** ______________________

2.

HEDRICK COMPANY
Comparative Income Statements

	This Year	Last Year

3. Comments:

Problem 17-14 Name ______________________

a. Market price of common stock:

b. Earnings per share:

c. Price-earnings ratio:

d. Financial leverage:

Problem 17-14 (Continued) Name ____________________

e. Company's ability to pay bills as they come due:

f. Customers' payment of bills as compared to last year:

g. Total of accounts receivable:

h. Level of inventory:

Problem 17-15 Name ______________________

Effect on Ratio	Reason for Increase, Decrease or No Effect
1.	
2.	
3.	
4.	
5.	

Problem 17-15 (Continued)   Name ____________________

Effect on Ratio	Reason for Increase, Decrease or No Effect
6.	
7.	
8.	
9.	
10.	

Effect on Ratio	Reason for Increase, Decrease or No Effect
11.	
12.	
13.	
14.	
15.	

 Name ______________________

Effect on Ratio	Reason for Increase, Decrease or No Effect
16.	
17.	
18.	

Problem 17-16 Name ______________________

1.

	This Year	Last Year
a. Earnings per share:		
b. Dividend yield ratio:		
c. Dividend payout ratio:		
d. Price-earnings ratio:		
e. Book values per share of common stock:		
f. Gross margin percentage:		

 Name ____________________

2.

	This Year	Last Year
a. Return on total assets:		
b. Return on common stockholders' equity:		

c. Comments regarding financial leverage:

3. Comments regarding attractiveness of common stock as an investment:

Problem 17-17 Name ____________________

1.

	This Year	Last Year
a. Working capital:		
b. Current ratio:		
c. Acid-test ratio:		
d. Average collection period:		
e. Inventory turnover:		
f. Times interest earned:		
g. Debt-to-equity ratio:		

Problem 17-17 (Continued) Name ______________________

2. Comments regarding company's current financial condition:

3. Comments regarding approval of loan:

Problem 17-18 Name ______________________

1. Income Statements in common-size format:

	This Year	Last Year
	%	%

2. Balance Sheets in common-size format:

	%	%

Problem 17-18 (Continued) **Name** ____________________

2. Comments regarding cost-cutting efforts:

Problem 17-19 Name ____________________

TANNER COMPANY
Income Statement
For the Year Ended December 31

TANNER COMPANY
Balance Sheet
December 31

(Note: The following pages are provided for our computations.)

Problem 17-19 (Continued) Name ______________________

Computations:

 Name ______________________

Computations, continued:

Problem 17-19 (Continued) Name

Computations, continued:

Problem 17-20 **Name** ____________________

1. Comments regarding company's ability to qualify for loan:

Problem 17-20 (Continued) Name

2. Advice:

Group Exercise 17-21 **Name** ______________________

Group Exercise 17-21 (Continued) Name ______________________

Problem A-5 Name ______________________

1. Contribution margin:

	$5 Price	$6 Price

2. Price elasticity of demand:

3. Profit-maximizing price:

Problem A-5 (Continued) **Name** ______________________

Problem A-5 (Continued) **Name** ______________________

Price	Quantity Sold	Sales	Cost of Sales	Contribution Margin

Problem A-5 (Continued) **Name** ______________________________

Contribution margin as a function of the selling price:

 Name

4. Profit-maximizing price and comments:

Problem A-6 **Name** ____________________

1. a. Markup percentage on absorption cost:

b. Target selling price:

c. Income statement

ROI:

2. Variable cost per unit:

Comments:

Problem A-7 **Name** ______________________

1. Target cost:

Maximum allowable purchase price for machine:

(Note: Part 2 is on the next page.)

Problem A-7 (Continued) Name ______________________

2. Relation between purchase price and ROI:

ROI for purchase prices between $2,400 and $3,400:

Problem A-7 (Continued) **Name** ______________________

Relation between purchase price and ROI:

Problem A-7 (Continued) Name ______________________

3. Options:

Problem A-8 **Name** ______________________

1. a. and b.

Parts: Material Loading Charge	
%	
Total	

Reports	
Per Hour	
Total	

Problem A-8 (Continued)   Name ____________________

2. Total price of job:

3. Comments:

Problem A-9 **Name** ______________________________

1.

Selling Price	Estimated Unit Sales	Sales	Variable Cost	Fixed	Net Operating Income

Problem A-9 (Continued) **Name** ______________________

2. Graph:

3. Price elasticity of demand:

Profit-maximizing price:

 Name

4. Target selling price and effect on net operating income if this price was charged:

5. Recommendation regarding selling price:

Problem A-10 **Name** ______________________

1. Supporting computations:

Standard cost card:

	Standard Quantity or Hours	Standard Price or Rate	Standard Cost

2. a. Markup percentage on absorption cost:

Problem A-10 **Name** ______________________

b. Target selling price:

c. Net operating income:

ROI:

Problem A-10 (Continued) Name ______________________

3. Break-even point in units sold: